100 Westerns

100 WESTERNS

BFI Screen Guides

Edward Buscombe

First published in 2006 by the
British Film Institute
21 Stephen Street, London W1T 1LN

The British Film Institute's purpose is to champion moving image culture in all its
richness and diversity across the UK, for the benefit of as wide an audience as
possible, and to create and encourage debate.

Series over design: Paul Wright
Cover image: *The Outlaw Josey Wales* (Clint Eastwood, 1976, © Warner Bros.)
Series design: Ketchup/couch
Set by Fakenham Photosetting Limited, Fakenham, Norfolk
Printed in the UK by The Cromwell Press, Trowbridge, Wiltshire

British Library Cataloguing-in-Publication Data
A catalogue record for this book is available from the British Library

ISBN 1–84457–112–2 (pbk)
ISBN 1–84457–111–4 (hbk)

Contents

Introduction

For many decades the Western occupied a central position within the American film industry. From around 1910 until the beginning of the 1960s, films in the Western genre made up at least a fifth of all titles released. No other genre has ever occupied anything like such a dominant position.

Within such a large body of material (maybe about 7,000 Westerns in all), there were bound to be great variations, both in the nature of the films and in their quality. Many of those produced, especially in the 20s, 30s and 40s, were cheaply made B-features, designed for the bottom half of a double bill, or else series Westerns, made by specialist units starring performers who were dedicated to the genre and targeted at audiences such as children and the patrons of small rural cinemas. These films were made to a formula, and in the interests of economy but also of giving their audiences what they knew and liked, they confined themselves to a relatively small number of stock situations.

Within the A-feature Western, with major stars, there was a greater range of material. The west of America was a large place, home to a wide range of human activity. It is true that the history in which the genre is grounded occupied a comparatively short period of time. Most Westerns taking place at a specified date are set in the period between the end of the Civil War and about 1890, when the historian Frederick Jackson Turner famously pronounced that the frontier, the line between settled and unsettled country, no longer existed. Yet within that period, scarcely a generation, we find stories of goldmining and cattle-ranching, of struggles against the Indian, stories of railroad-building and pioneering, tales of notorious outlaws and equally celebrated lawmen.

The Western is protean. It readily adapts itself to other genres. There are Western comedies and musicals, Western films noirs, pornographic Westerns, even Western science-fiction and horror films (*Jesse James Meets Frankenstein's Daughter* [1965], believe it or not). Some of the B-features of the 1940s are set in World War II, with the heroes battling against Nazis or Japanese spies. And from the earliest days the genre was transplanted from America, taking root in several European countries. French companies were making Westerns in the Camargue in the early 1910s, while Germans made Westerns in the 1920s, and then again in the 1960s, with both East and West Germany turning out a string of titles shot in spectacular mountain locations, some with imported American stars. As everyone knows, the Italians followed suit later in the decade, ultimately producing several hundred 'spaghetti' Westerns.

Inevitably, over the lengthy history of the genre, the Western has changed, though not necessarily in a straightforward line of development. For example, back in the early silent days, stories of Indians were highly popular, many of them set at a time or in a place where whites are absent. Such stories, owing much to literary origins such as Henry Wadsworth Longfellow's poem *Hiawatha* (1855), offered a sympathetic if idealised and at times condescending portrayal of Indian life. But these stories had fallen from favour by the 1920s, and it was not until the 1950s, perhaps as a result of campaigns over Civil Rights, possibly because of shifting perceptions of race in the light of World War II, that films with favourable depictions of Indians began once again to appear in significant numbers.

The position of women within the Western was always slow to reflect changes in the wider society. Issues of masculinity have been central to the genre, and though this need not preclude strong roles for women, they have in practice been few and far between. Again, one can find examples of feisty heroines in some early silent films, far in advance of women's roles in films of the 1940s or 1950s. Unfortunately, just at the time in the later 1960s when race and gender became key social issues which mainstream social institutions ignored at their peril, the Western, perhaps not coincidentally, entered its long decline, to the point where the genre now appears a threatened species, preserved only in occasional self-conscious attempts to retool it for contemporary audiences.

Though Hollywood no longer appears to believe there is a steady audience for the Western movie, elsewhere in the culture the idea of the west retains its potency. History books on the American west pour forth in greater numbers than ever. In music and in fashion, the west retains its appeal. In serious fiction, the west, both as an idea and as a real place, is a resource mined by writers as varied as Larry McMurtry, Cormac McCarthy, James Crumley, Sam Shepard and E. Annie Proulx. And, paradoxically, the Western film itself now attracts more critical writing than ever, with the number of books on the genre published each year exceeding the number of Westerns released.

Given this volume of scholarly literature, there is no need here to offer an outline of the 100-year history of the Western, nor provide a definition of the genre, nor attempt to trace the manifold connections between the Western and American history, nor its relation to cultural and social forces. Instead, I shall offer some comments on the principles which have guided the selection of a mere 100 films from the thousands which make up the complete corpus.

These 100 are not necessarily my favourite films, the ones which I should most like to see again. That's not to say I haven't enjoyed seeing all of them very much, but there are probably another 100 films I would enjoy equally, or nearly so. Given that fact, I have tried to make a representative selection. In the first place, all of the great directors of the Western have several titles included. Foremost in the pantheon is John Ford, who has no less than nine films to his name. Some may find this excessive, but that Ford is pre-eminent among the directors associated with the genre is undeniable, and several excellent Ford films, such as *Drums along the Mohawk* (1939), *3 Godfathers* (1948), *Sergeant Rutledge* (1960) and *Cheyenne Autumn* (1964), have been omitted.

However, when I set out to compile the list I did not consciously rank directors in my mind and decide in advance how many films by each should be included. It was therefore with some surprise I discovered, when I had assembled the list, that the director with the next highest number was Delmer Daves, who has five films to represent him, compared to only four for Anthony Mann, Sam Peckinpah, Howard Hawks, Clint Eastwood and Sergio Leone. I do not believe that Daves is a better director than these others (though he is certainly a better director than he has been given credit for). I think the reason for Daves' unexpected eminence may be that each of his films selected has something else besides the excellence of the direction to recommend it; an outstanding performance by a star, perhaps, or an important place within the history of the genre. *Broken Arrow* (1950) would qualify on both counts.

These statistics on the relative status of directors may in fact show that, despite the persistence of the idea of the auteur within film criticism, the Western genre may amount to something more than the sum of the work of great directors. This productive tension between auteur and genre is explored with great insight by Jim Kitses in the new, expanded version of his classic study, *Horizons West*. As far as this book is concerned, it will be apparent that the director's name is not the only principle which has guided selection. Some films have demanded inclusion because they stand for an important development in the history of the genre, or because they mark a particularly interesting relationship between the Western and American society.

Of all the directors who have made a significant contribution to the genre, perhaps Budd Boetticher is the one who may feel most aggrieved, with a mere three films in the selection. I think that if I were allowed one extra title, it would probably be Boetticher's *Seven Men from Now* (1956), which has all the virtues of his other classic films. By contrast, Clint Eastwood, the most recent of the directors in the pantheon, has in fact a larger presence in the book than his four titles as director would suggest, since he is also a major force in films directed by Don Siegel and Sergio Leone.

Leaving aside the question of directors, what other issues have guided the selection? As far as performers are concerned, I didn't consciously set out to ensure that the major stars were represented proportionately to their importance, though it will come as no surprise that John Wayne has the most titles (ten), followed by Clint Eastwood with eight and James Stewart with seven. Gary Cooper may be thought under-represented with a mere three titles, as may Kirk Douglas. My own favourite Western star, for what it's worth, is Randolph Scott, who graced many small-budget films with his dignified and stoical performances, and he has four titles in the list, alongside Henry Fonda, Robert Mitchum and Burt Lancaster.

I have tried, within the limits of space, to give some sense of the history of the genre. While the great majority of films are from the 1940s, 50s and 60s, undoubtedly its heyday, there is at least one film from every decade of the Western's existence. I do not pretend that there is an adequate representation of the silent period, because many films from that era no longer exist, and even the ones that do are not always generally available. Nor have I chosen many films from the series or B-feature Western, despite its overwhelming presence in terms of sheer numbers produced. But in drawing attention to such titles as *Oh, Susanna!* (1936) and *Terror in a Texas Town* (1958) I have tried to indicate that the Western amounts to more than John Ford and Sam Peckinpah.

I have also given some weight to Westerns made outside Hollywood. From the very beginning, as I have already indicated, the Western proved popular in virtually every country of the world. The way was prepared by the torrent of dime novels that poured from the presses in the later years of the nineteenth century, and which circulated abroad in translation, stimulating a mass appetite for tales of daring and adventure set in the American west. Buffalo Bill Cody, himself a hero of hundreds of such publications, built upon their popularity, touring Europe several times with his 'Wild West', a combination of rodeo, circus and theatre that brought to a world audience the stock characters of cowboy and Indian and many of the narrative situations (capture by Indians, an attack on a stagecoach) which the cinema would soon reproduce in countless films. The west as a subject for entertainment found Europe in particular a fertile ground, and in due course a crop of home-grown Westerns was produced, some of them strange mutations indeed. It's also worth noting that because of the international currency of the west, it's no surprise that so many foreign-born directors in Hollywood should have been drawn to the genre. Fred Zinnemann, Fritz Lang, Jacques Tourneur, André de Toth, Michael Curtiz, all European-born, are each represented here.

Part of the fun of canon-formation, the making of lists of who or what is most significant, is in comparing one's own selection with those of others. I would be surprised if many people would come up with a hundred Western titles that would exactly match my own. That is as it should be. This list makes no pretensions to authority. I have seen each of these films again in the course of writing this book and I stand by my selections as all eminently worth ninety minutes or so of anyone's time. But there are many excellent and significant films that did not squeeze in, and it is not my intention to exclude them from future recognition, only to bring my selections to the reader's attention.

The Western celebrated its centenary in 2003. Since then, the number of Westerns which Hollywood has produced can probably be numbered on the fingers of one hand. A generation has grown up who find John Wayne's Western machismo a little over the top. It's not that audiences don't want action heroes; indeed, contemporary mass cinema might be considered over-supplied in that department. But Wayne and many other Western stars of the past lack the ironic, wise-cracking manner that modern audiences prefer. For today's filmgoers, the Western seems hamstrung by its historical setting, handicapped by its primitive technology, by its period costumes and its quaintly old-fashioned manners. Moreover, many in the audience have lost the folk memory which would allow them to understand the conventions upon which the genre depends for narrative coherence; they have lost the basic ability to read the films.

I cannot pretend to any great optimism that Hollywood will rediscover the Western. Other genres have moved in to fill the space it once occupied. What is certain, however, is that the cinema's past is now more in circulation than it has ever been. The explosive growth, first of video and now of the DVD market, has made available hundreds of cinema classics that had lapsed into obscurity. Now, once again, great films of the past can be seen, with the maximum of convenience and, within the limitations of the home, in something approximating the technical state their directors would wish. At last we can see the great CinemaScope Westerns of the 1950s in their correct ratio, we can see Technicolor restored, we can even see integrated back into the films sequences which were taken out against the director's wishes. A significant number of the best films ever made in Hollywood were Westerns, and there has never been a better time for appreciating them. If this book has one single ambition, it is to provide a helpful guide, both for those who know the Western genre and for those who do not, suggesting which films will most repay viewing or re-viewing. In my opinion.

Bibliography

Christopher Frayling, *Spaghetti Westerns* (London: Routledge & Kegan Paul, 1981).

Eric Hobsbawm, *Bandits* (New York: The New Press, 2000).

Jim Kitses, *Horizons West* (London: BFI, 2004).

Andrew Sarris, *The American Cinema: Directors and Directions 1929–1968* (New York: Dutton, 1968).

Across the Wide Missouri
US, 1950 – 78 mins
William Wellman

The title of the film, and some elements of the story, are based upon a
book by Bernard DeVoto, a history of the mountain men in the 1830s. In
the book DeVoto tells the story of William Drummond Stewart, a
Scotsman, a former officer in the British army and a keen sportsman,
who undertook a journey up the Missouri River in 1837. Accompanying
Stewart was a young painter, Alfred Jacob Miller, whose pictures would
provide Stewart with souvenirs of his hunting trip. These two characters
survive into William Wellman's film, though with only marginal roles and
with the names changed. The hero is Flint Mitchell (Clark Gable), an
experienced mountain man and trapper who plans an expedition into the
dangerous but rich beaver country of the Blackfoot Indians in the
Rockies. In order to assist his relations with the Indians he is persuaded to
marry a young Blackfoot woman, Kamiah (María Elena Marqués), who
wishes to return to her tribe. Encountering resistance from Indians along
the trail, Kamiah takes the party on a route across the high mountains.
They settle in the Blackfoot country and build a fort, enjoying good
relations with Kamiah's grandfather Bear Ghost (Jack Holt), but the
young warrior Ironshirt (Ricardo Montalban) is hostile. One of the
trappers is killed and his brother shoots Bear Ghost in revenge, leading to
further hostilities. In the spring Kamiah has a baby and the trappers
prepare to leave, but are attacked by Indians and Kamiah is killed. The
horse carrying the infant bolts and Ironshirt chases it with Flint in pursuit.
After killing Ironshirt, Flint decides to return with his son to the Blackfoot
country.

The film can be seen as part of a cycle of pro-Indian films from the
early 1950s, including *Broken Arrow* (1950) and *Devil's Doorway* (1950).
At first Flint has no great respect for Indians, rudely turning Kamiah away
when she makes overtures. But he is won over by her charm, and when
he gets to know Bear Ghost he begins to see Indians as, in the words of

the voice-over commentary supplied in retrospect by his son, 'people with hopes and traditions and ways of their own. Suddenly, they were no longer savages.' Gradually he learns to speak a little of Kamiah's language, as she does his. The film is remarkable in allowing both Indians and the Frenchmen among the trappers to speak their native tongues (though whether what the Indians speak is actually Blackfoot is questionable). As in other Westerns of the period, pro-Indian attitudes only extend so far. The good Indian/bad Indian dichotomy prevails, good Indians being those who are friendly to the whites. But at the end, although the racial mixing of the marriage is cut short, as in *Broken Arrow*, Flint decides that his son should have a Blackfoot education before a white one.

Despite some splendid mountain scenery and a spirited performance by Gable, the film proved unpopular with preview audiences and was savagely cut to its present length of barely seventy-five minutes.

Dir: William Wellman; **Prod**: Robert Sisk; **Scr**: Talbot Jennings; **DOP**: William C. Mellor; **Score**: David Raksin.

Antonio das Mortes/Dragao da maldade contra o santo guerreiro
Brazil, 1969 – 95 mins
Glauber Rocha

An extraordinary product of the Cinema Novo movement in Brazil, Glauber Rocha's film is a strange, at times delirious, folktale which draws upon the tradition of social banditry in the sertão, the desert region of north-east Brazil which has traditionally been the poorest part of the country. (Social banditry as described by the historian Eric Hobsbawm refers to figures such as Robin Hood who, though outlaws, are supported by the poor because they prey only on their oppressors.) In this respect the film has something in common with Westerns about Jesse James or Billy the Kid, in which the outlaw is a tragic figure who acts as the focus of social discontent. However, Rocha's film is quite unlike Hollywood in its visual style or in the nature of its narrative. The central character, Antonio das Mortes, or Antonio of Death (Mauricio do Valle), had in fact appeared in an earlier Rocha film, *Black God, White Devil* (1964). At the beginning he is in retirement but is requested to come and kill Coirana (Lorival Pariz), who has inherited the mantle of Lampião, a celebrated *cangaceiro* or bandit. A long, highly stylised fight ensues, but although Coirana is killed, Antonio undergoes a political conversion, realising that Coirana stands for the cause of the oppressed peasantry. Antonio begins a campaign against Mata Vaca (Vinicius Salvatore), who has been brought in by the Colonel (Jofre Soares), a tyrannical local landowner, to deal with the landless peasants who are in revolt. Mata Vaca leads a group of killers called the *jaguncos*. Antonio forms an alliance with a teacher (Othon Bastos) who, like him, has changed sides to support the peasants. In a final battle, Antonio and the teacher, together with mythical figures from religious folklore, defeat Mata Vaca and the *jaguncos* and kill the Colonel.

Rocha drew deliberately on the tradition of the American Western for his climactic sequence:

> I wanted to recapture the spirit of a Western I had seen, *Ride the High
> Country*, as I was very attached to the image of Randolph Scott and Joel
> McCrea firing side by side at the end of the film.

And Antonio has something in common with the characters played by
Clint Eastwood in his Italian Westerns, a mercenary with a distinctive
sartorial style (Eastwood has his serape, Antonio his hat), who at first
works for the bad guys but then switches sides. Rocha's style is even
more operatic than Leone's, with highly theatrical acting and
exaggerated, comic-book violence. The film operates as an allegory of
Brazil at the time the film was made, with the *jaguncos* as forerunners of
the later death squads and the *cangaceiros* as proto-typical guerrillas.
Overlaid on the political message, however, is a layer of mysticism, with
the figure of St George frequently invoked, together with elements of
African religion represented in the form of Ogum. An interesting
experiment which has something in common with another Latin
American pseudo-Western of the period, Jodorowsky's *El Topo* (1971).

Dir: Glauber Rocha; **Prod**: Glauber Rocha, Claude Antoine Mapa; **Scr**: Glauber Rocha;
DOP: Alfonso Beato; **Score**: Marlos Nobre, Walter Queiroz, Sergio Ricardo.

Apache
US, 1954 – 91 mins
Robert Aldrich

One of a group of films from the early 1950s, including *Broken Arrow* (1950) and *Across the Wide Missouri* (1950), that take a more sympathetic view of the Indians than in earlier Westerns, *Apache* is scripted by James R. Webb, who ten years later would write *Cheyenne Autumn*, John Ford's pro-Indian Western. The six-foot, blue-eyed Burt Lancaster makes an unlikely Indian, even in a black wig, but the film is very much a starring vehicle for the actor, who was one of the first in Hollywood to form his own production company, together with his agent Harold Hecht. The film begins with the surrender of Geronimo (Monte Blue) in 1886. Massai (Lancaster) declares that Geronimo does not speak for him and that he will fight on. Though captured and put on a train to Florida with the other Apaches, he escapes somewhere in the mid-west. A cleverly conceived sequence shows him gazing in amazement at the trappings of white city life: a Chinese laundry, ladies' bustles, a mechanical piano. On the way back to Arizona he meets a Cherokee farmer, who gives him some seed corn. Massai is contemptuous ('Apaches are warriors not farmers!'). Back on the reservation he shows the seeds to Nalinle (Jean Peters) and her father Santos (Paul Guilfoyle). Santos betrays him and he is sent back to Florida, but on the way he escapes once more, killing the oppressive Indian agent Weddle (John Dehner). Kidnapping Nalinle, who he believes also betrayed him, he goes deep into the wilderness, pursued by scout Al Sieber (John McIntire) and Hondo (Charles Bronson), a member of the Apache police who wishes to marry Nalinle. Eventually Massai's hostility to Nalinle turns to love and the couple conceive a child. They also grow corn from the seed Massai brought back from the mid-west. When their hiding place is discovered, Massai lays down his weapons after hearing the cries of his new-born child.

Director Robert Aldrich was prevailed upon to shoot alternative endings, in one of which Lancaster fights to the death, but the happy ending, not very convincing in view of Massai's repeated pronouncements that he is doomed, was preferred against the director's wishes. Up until that point the film has been an eloquent presentation of the rejectionist position which in *Broken Arrow* is put by Geronimo, that only through resistance can the Indians maintain their way of life. The Cherokee farmer puts the counter-view advocated by Cochise in *Broken Arrow*: 'We found that we could live with the white man only if we live like him.' Massai's espousal of traditional ways extends to a somewhat patriarchal view of women, though this is undercut with humour. Observing the Cherokee going to get water, Massai chides him: 'You have a woman and yet you carry the water?' The Cherokee shrugs resignedly: 'Some of the white man's ways are hard.' And when Nalinle observes that a rabbit he has caught is rather small, Massai's reply shows up his comic pomposity: 'It is for me to decide if it is large or small.'

Dir: Robert Aldrich; **Prod**: Harold Hecht; **Scr**: James R. Webb; **DOP**: Ernest Laszlo; **Score**: David Raksin.

The Battle at Elderbush Gulch
US, 1913 – 29 mins
D. W. Griffith

D. W. Griffith made dozens of Westerns during his time at the Biograph studio; indeed, the genre comprised nearly fifteen per cent of all the films produced there from 1908 to 1912. The stories concerned Indians, Mexicans, miners, trappers and other stock characters of the genre. Some of the films involving Indians are set in a period prior to the arrival of whites, or at a distant remove from them, and several of these take the form of love stories, such as *The Song of the Wildwood Flute* (1910), in which a jealous rival for the love of Little Dove attacks her husband, Grey Cloud, imprisoning him in a bear trap before remorsefully releasing him. However, Griffith apparently found no contradiction between making films that celebrated an idyllic Indian existence and filming stories in which the Indians are primitive savages whose defeat, and even extermination, was essential to the progress of the whites.

By 1913, the budgets for Griffith's films were getting substantially bigger and their length was increasing (*The Birth of a Nation* was only two years away). The director was beginning to impose on the Western the broad expansive sweep which would ultimately result in the epic Westerns of the early 1920s such as *The Covered Wagon* (1923) and *The Iron Horse* (1924). In *The Battle at Elderbush Gulch* Griffith cast two of his favourite actresses, Lillian Gish and Mae Marsh. The former is a young mother who has come west by stagecoach with her husband and baby. Mae Marsh is Sally, a 'waif'. A nearby tribe of Indians become drunk and go in search of the dog meat they like to eat. When they take the pets of the settlers, the whites retaliate and the chief's son is killed. The Indians go on the warpath and attack the white settlement. A furious battle ensues, during which Gish, her baby and the waif take refuge in one of the houses. The Indians come near to breaking in, threatening the women with a fate worse than death. Griffith employs his favoured technique for heightening tension by constructing parallel actions, in this case the Indians almost breaking through the settlers' defences while the cavalry rides to the rescue. In what was, if not already a convention of the genre then shortly to become so, a white woman is advised to save the last bullet for herself.

There's an absolute gulf in the film between the whites, portrayed in idealistic terms, nurturing their children and their puppies alike, and the Indians, drunken savages who not only murder without mercy but, perhaps worse still, eat dogs by choice. But despite the obvious racism (a charge which was to be renewed when *The Birth of a Nation* appeared), the film has an exciting narrative sweep and a genuinely exciting climax, something which later film-makers would gratefully build upon.

Dir: D. W. Griffith; **Prod**: n/a; **Scr**: D. W. Griffith; **DOP**: Billy Bitzer.

The Beguiled
US, 1970 – 105 mins
Don Siegel

The original script for *The Beguiled* was written by Albert Maltz, one of the blacklisted Hollywood Ten who had also written *Two Mules for Sister Sara* (1970), the previous collaboration between director Don Siegel and star Clint Eastwood. But Maltz wanted a happy ending. Siegel found this too sentimental and preferred a far darker conclusion, faithful to Thomas Cullinan's original novel. The story is set in the Civil War. A wounded Union soldier, John McBurney (Eastwood) is discovered by twelve-year-old Amy (Pamelyn Ferdin), a pupil at a girl's seminary somewhere in the Confederate south. The school is owned by Martha (Geraldine Page), assisted by a young teacher, Edwina (Elizabeth Hartman). They take McBurney in and care for him, but only until he is well enough to be taken off to prison. Isolated from men for the duration of the war, all the women are in a state of febrile sexual anticipation. McBurney can't believe his luck and embarks on a series of flirtations, with the two white women, with the black maid Hallie (Mae Mercer) and with Carol (Jo Ann Harris), a precociously amorous pupil. McBurney's adventures go disastrously wrong when he is surprised in Carol's bed by Edwina, who has fallen in love with him. In the ensuing fracas McBurney breaks his wounded leg. In an apparent act of vicious revenge for the fact that he did not come to her bed as he had promised, Martha decrees that his leg must be amputated to avoid gangrene. But McBurney has still not learned his lesson and continues to treat the women as his personal playthings. On the night before his departure they cook a special dinner, at which he is served poisoned mushrooms.

On one hand, it could be argued that this is not, strictly speaking, a Western at all, but rather an example of Southern Gothic. On the other hand, there is a long tradition of Civil War pictures, such as John Ford's *The Horse Soldiers* (1959), with close connections to the mainstream of the Western genre. And although an unusual subject for Eastwood, the film fits in right at the centre of his oeuvre. The theme of 'a woman scorned' is taken up in Eastwood's next film, *Play Misty for Me* (1971), his first as director. It's also interesting in terms of the development of Eastwood's screen persona, which, though ostensibly macho, is often slyly subverted by women who prove to be his match, or nearly so. McBurney reveals himself to be a manipulative liar, pretending to be a Quaker drafted into the army against his principles, in order to curry favour with the southern belles, while, as a strategy of seduction, suggesting to Hallie that they are both on the same side. He quickly searches out sexual secrets (Martha has had an incestuous affair with her brother, Edwina's father was a lecher), but seals his fate with his contemptuous treatment of them all. His mocking recital of grace at his last supper (there have been Christ-like images in Martha's mind) is a fitting prelude to his come-uppance; in all, a wonderfully acted and atmospheric film.

Dir: Don Siegel; **Prod**: Don Siegel; **Scr**: John B. Sherry [Albert Maltz], Grimes Grice [Irene Kamp]; **DOP**: Bruce Surtees; **Score**: Lalo Schifrin.

The Big Sky
US, 1952 – 122 mins
Howard Hawks

A. B. Guthrie Jr was a Montana newspaperman whose first major novel was *The Big Sky*. Guthrie later went to Hollywood and wrote the script for *Shane* (1953), based on Jack Schaefer's novella. Other Guthrie novels to become Western films were *The Way West* and *These Thousand Hills*, which detailed the further adventures of some of the characters in *The Big Sky*. In fashioning the script, Hawks and his screenwriter Dudley Nichols (who had written *Stagecoach* [1939] for John Ford) worked up Guthrie's rambling narrative into a familiar Hawksian tale of a 'love story' between two men. In the 1830s, Jim Deakins (Kirk Douglas) and Boone Caudill (Dewey Martin) meet by chance and travel to St Louis together, where they encounter Boone's uncle Zeb (Arthur Hunnicutt). The three of them enlist in a venture by riverboat up the Missouri in order to trade in furs with the Blackfoot Indians. Their guarantee that the Indians will be friendly comes in the form of Teal Eye (Elizabeth Threatt), a Blackfoot princess kidnapped from her people, whom the traders will take back home. Along the way they have to fight off attempts by the monopoly fur company to scupper their enterprise. The friendship between Jim and Boone is sorely tested when each of them falls for Teal Eye (in the novel she was only twelve, but Hawks increased her age to make her the centre of the love interest). Eventually, though regarding Jim as a brother, she takes Boone as her lover and, after some hesitation, he decides to stay behind with the Blackfoot when the traders depart back down river.

Hawks did not regard the film as one of his favourites, for a variety of reasons. It was cut by the studio on release (apparently a longer version, at 140 minutes, exists), the film did only moderately at the box office, and Kirk Douglas was not Hawks's first choice for Jim Deakins, the director preferring John Wayne or Gary Cooper. Nevertheless, this is a fine example of the mountain man subgenre, and Douglas gives a spirited performance. Hawks managed to persuade him to do a scene which Wayne had refused to do in *Red River* (1947), in which his damaged finger is amputated, the entire scene being played as black comedy. Elizabeth Threatt, half-Cherokee, is not required to do much more than look pretty in her only film appearance, and Dewey Martin is rather over-extended as Boone, but Arthur Hunnicutt holds things together as the garrulous, hard-drinking Zeb, teller of tall tales.

As with several films of this period, *The Big Sky* makes earnest efforts to resist racism. Zeb attacks the covetousness of the whites ('White men don't see nothing pretty but they want to grab it'), while the Blackfoot prove hospitable. The Indian Poor Devil (Hank Worden), though touched in the head, is loyal and kindly, and Boone, who begins by hating Indians (he carries the scalp of an Indian who killed his brother) is at last won round by Teal Eye's charms.

Dir: Howard Hawks; **Prod**: Howard Hawks; **Scr**: Dudley Nichols; **DOP**: Russell Harlan; **Score**: Dimitri Tiomkin.

The Big Trail
US, 1930 – 110 mins
Raoul Walsh

Dedicated to 'the men and women who planted civilization in the wilderness', this is an ambitious film on a large scale. It is also John Wayne's first starring role, nearly a decade before *Stagecoach* (1939). It's not quite the Wayne we are used to; here, he's a bit gauche, but slim, lissom and rather charming in the role of Breck Coleman, the scout of a wagon train going west to Oregon in the 1830s. The plot is similar to *The Covered Wagon*, a big hit in 1923, though *The Big Trail* is greatly superior in execution. Breck has a romance with Ruth (Marguerite Churchill), who is also being courted by Thorpe (Ian Keith), who claims to have a plantation down south but is in fact a cheap gambler. Breck is seeking the men who murdered his friend out in the wild, and suspects Flack (Tyrone Power), the leader of the wagon train, and his rascally sidekick Lopez (Charles Stevens). Along the trail, after surviving attempts to kill him, Breck finds the evidence he needs against Flack and Lopez. He tracks them through a blizzard and justice is finally done.

The romance is tedious, dragged out by a series of misunderstandings; at one point Ruth throws a tantrum because she thinks Breck's Indian friends, who are trading horses, are buying her as a squaw for him. The acting styles are not always adapted to the new medium of sound film. Tyrone Power in particular, with a voice like a sand-blaster and energetic eye-rolling, appears to have strayed in from the provincial Victorian stage. Attempts at comedy with a Scandinavian family, funny accents and all, fall flat. But the location shooting is on an epic scale. The wagon train is immense and the oxen used to pull the wagons give it an authentic appearance. When the wagons ford a river the threat to life and limb looks very real. There are buffalo stampedes and snowstorms, and a large-scale Indian attack, with the wagons in a circle, as tradition demands. Most spectacular of all is a sequence in which the entire wagon train has to be lowered down the side of a steep

Lowering the wagons down a cliff – a spectacular scene from *The Big Trail*

cliff, oxen and all. Shot in a new process, named Fox Grandeur, a 70mm format, not wide-screen but with greatly enhanced resolution, the film is a triumph of realistic staging.

The film swallows the myth of Manifest Destiny whole, with Breck making an inspirational speech to rally the settlers when they are at a low ebb: 'We're blazing a trail that started in England . . . we're building a nation.' Unfortunately the film did not do well at the box office. At the height of the Depression few theatres could afford to install the new equipment required for the 70mm version. Consequently John Wayne's career went into eclipse and he languished in the B-feature Western for the rest of the decade until John Ford rescued him for *Stagecoach*.

Dir: Raoul Walsh; **Prod**: Winfield R. Sheehan; **Scr**: Jack Peabody, Marie Boyle, Florence Postal, Fred Serser; **DOP**: Lucien Andriot, Arthur Edeson; **Score**: Arthur Kay.

Broken Arrow
US, 1950 – 93 mins
Delmer Daves

In the 1950s, possibly resulting from the political legacy of the fight
against Fascism in World War II, possibly because of the beginnings of
Civil Rights agitation, Hollywood made a series of films which attempted
a sympathetic portrayal of Indians. Instead of the screaming savages who
had filled the screen hitherto, there were Indian heroes: wise, brave,
honourable. Among these films, *Broken Arrow* has become a landmark.
Although originally credited on screen to Michael Blankfort, the film was
written by the blacklisted Albert Maltz, a former Communist. Based upon
real-life events dating from the 1870s, the film is told in flashback by its
hero, Tom Jeffords (James Stewart), an army scout who, at first

Broken Arrow: Sonseeahray (Debra Paget) in her wedding dress, with Tom Jeffords (James
Stewart), Cochise (Jeff Chandler) and Nalikadeya (Argentina Brunetti)

unsympathetic, is converted to the cause of the Chiricahua Apaches
under their chief Cochise. Following the custom of the time, Cochise is
played by a tall, dark and handsome white actor, Jeff Chandler.
Becoming familiar with Apache ways, even to the extent of learning their
language, Jeffords falls in love with an Apache woman, Sonseeahray
(also played by a white actor, Debra Paget). Jeffords negotiates a peace
settlement between Cochise and the army under General Howard.
Popularly known as 'the Christian general', Howard remarks at one point
that, 'My Bible says nothing about the pigmentation of the skin'. In a key
scene Jeffords explains to Cochise that the Apache will be settled on a
reservation and given tools and stock to enable them to become farmers.
One faction of the tribe, under Geronimo (played by Native American
actor, Jay Silverheels, as a bitter, snarling troublemaker), rejects the offer,
accusing Cochise of being weak. Cochise's response is unequivocal:

> The Americans keep cattle, but they are not soft or weak. Why should not the
> Apache be able to learn new ways? It is not easy to change but sometimes it
> is required. The Americans are growing stronger while we are growing
> weaker. If a big wind comes, a tree must bend, or be lifted out by its roots.

The liberal position of the film depends on viewing at least some of the
Apaches as reasonable human beings, but this extends only to those
who accept the process of assimilation, which was the policy of the US
government at the time in which the film is set and for much of the
twentieth century. Indians were expected eventually to integrate into the
wider American society and give up their distinctive culture. In practice,
despite the manifold disadvantages suffered by the Indian population,
this has not happened.

The film's liberalism is also compromised by the fate of Sonseeahray,
who at the end of the film is murdered by whites, thus nipping in the
bud the potentially subversive theme of miscegenation. In this the film is
not alone; very few of the mixed-race relationships in Westerns ever end
happily. Despite this, the film adds to its good intentions the virtues of

excellent acting, particularly by Stewart, pleasing colour photography and efficient direction by Delmer Daves, whose first Western it was.

Dir: Delmer Daves; **Prod**: Julian Blaustein; **Scr**: Albert Maltz; **DOP**: Ernest Palmer; **Score**: Hugo Friedhofer.

A Bullet for the General/Quien sabe?
Italy, 1966 – 135 mins
Damiano Damiani

One of the best examples of the so-called 'political' strain within the spaghetti Western, *A Bullet for the General* is dominated by the barnstorming performance of Gian Maria Volonté as El Chuncho, a Mexican bandit who steals guns from the army and sells them to the revolutionaries. Set during the period 1910 to 20 when Mexico was in turmoil, the film begins with an attack on a train, during which El Chuncho meets up with Tate (Lou Castel), a baby-faced gringo whom he names Niño. The figure of the foreign adviser, skilled in weapons technology and tactics, is a common one both in the spaghetti Western and in Hollywood films of the era such as *The Wild Bunch* (1969), and Tate, impeccably dressed in suit, collar and tie, helps the bandits attack a fort and steal weapons. Reserved in his demeanour, Tate begins to conduct a romance with Adelita (Martine Beswick), a female revolutionary, but in a half-hearted manner. When asked by El Chuncho what really interests him, he replies, 'Money.' By contrast, El Chuncho's brother El Santo (Klaus Kinski) is a former priest, a saintly figure (who doesn't realise El Chuncho is actually selling the guns), tossing grenades at the soldiers 'in the name of the Father – and of the Son – and of the Holy Ghost!'

El Chuncho takes them to San Miguel, where the bandits execute the local landowner Don Felipe (Andrea Checchi). Asked why, El Chuncho delivers his political credo: 'We are poor people; he wants us to stay poor people.' Tate wants to push on to the camp of General Elias (Jaime Fernández), who will buy their weapons, including a machine-gun they have acquired ('It's lovelier than any woman,' coos El Chuncho). At first reluctant to leave the peasants, whom he attempts to train as soldiers, El Chuncho eventually joins Tate and the others and they arrive at the camp of General Elias, where El Chuncho is accused of deserting the villagers of San Miguel, who have subsequently been massacred by counter-revolutionaries. But as El Chuncho is led out to be executed (his own brother volunteering for the task), Tate shoots both El Santo and the General, the latter with a golden bullet he had been hoarding for the purpose. Later, Tate is paid off by the Mexican government. He offers to share the money with El Chuncho but, as he is boarding a train to cross the border, El Chuncho shoots him.

Though, in the familiar Italian style, the film delivers its fair share of gun battles, with bullets incessantly zipping and whining on the soundtrack as bodies fall in droves, *A Bullet for the General* packs a genuine ideological punch, with the cold and calculating Tate a symbol of American machinations in Latin America, and the good-hearted if headstrong El Chuncho representing the not always fully formulated political aspirations of the Third World. What seems finally to arouse his anger against Tate is when the latter arrogantly pushes to the head of the queue at the station ticket office, a gesture of contempt towards the peasants standing in line.

Dir: Damiano Damiani; **Prod**: Bianco Manini; **Scr**: Salvatore Laurani; **DOP**: Toni Secchi; **Score**: Luis Enrique Bacalov.

Butch Cassidy and the Sundance Kid
US, 1969 – 110 mins
George Roy Hill

By 1983, this film had become the second most successful Western ever made in terms of US box-office receipts, outstripped only by *Blazing Saddles*. It's a clever film, slickly directed, which depends greatly on the charm of its two principal players. Butch Cassidy (Paul Newman) is the

Butch Cassidy (Paul Newman) and the Sundance Kid (Robert Redford) in a tight spot

leader of the Hole in the Wall Gang (the film has some basis in actual people and events). He is quick with repartee, always has an eye on the main chance and is never without a Big Idea. His friend the Sundance Kid (Robert Redford) is the quiet type, a romantic and a dead shot with a pistol. After defeating a rival for his leadership with a well-aimed kick in the groin, Butch leads the gang in a train hold-up. When they try to repeat the robbery, they are pursued by a posse. Narrowly escaping after hiding out in a brothel, they find the posse still relentlessly in pursuit. 'Who *are* those guys?' Butch remarks indignantly.

Butch proposes that they go to Bolivia in order to escape their pursuers. Once there, accompanied by Sundance's girlfriend Etta (Katharine Ross), they start robbing banks. At first it is easy, but their pursuers from America are still on their trail. Deciding to go straight they take a job as payroll guards for a mining company. But later they are recognised in a town which they have previously robbed. Surrounded by a large force of troops, they try to shoot their way out.

At certain points the film tells its story through a montage of sepia-coloured stills, designed to give it the patina of the early silent cinema period in which the action is set. But in fact the film is nothing if not of its time, with its smart, jokey tone and glossy look. At times it essays a meaningful commentary on its heroes' fate ('Your time is over and you're going to die bloody. All you can do is choose where,' says an old acquaintance), and there's an episode with a bicycle designed to show the old west is passing ('The horse is dead', the salesman claims). But Butch and Sundance are miles away from Peckinpah's *The Wild Bunch*, released the same year. For them, the west is a spree.

The film has some funny lines (Butch, exasperated by the dogged attempts of railroad baron E. H. Harriman to track them down, reasons: 'If he'd just pay me what he's spending to stop me robbing him, I'd stop robbing him.'). And there are some nicely judged comic scenes: Butch using too much dynamite on a safe, or trying to rob a Bolivian bank by reading out from a piece of paper the Spanish for 'Put your hands up'. There's also a wonderful little cameo by Peckinpah veteran Strother

Martin as a mine owner. But at times it's all a little too determinedly cheerful, not helped by Burt Bacharach's music, especially the awful 'Raindrops Keep Fallin' On My Head'.

Dir: George Roy Hill; **Prod**: John Foreman; **Scr**: William Goldman; **DOP**: Conrad Hall; **Score**: Burt Bacharach.

Calamity Jane
US, 1953 – 101 mins
David Butler

Music and the Western have gone hand in hand since the introduction of
sound. Singing cowboys, especially Gene Autry, became hugely popular
in the 1930s, while Jeanette MacDonald and Nelson Eddy had a big hit
with *Rose Marie* (1936). Many of the best-known musical Westerns have
been based on stage shows, including *Annie Get Your Gun* (1950) and
Oklahoma! (1955). *Calamity Jane* is an exception, with songs specially
written by Sammy Fain and Paul Francis Webster. Though 'Calamity Jane'
Canary did actually exist, the plot is based on the apocryphal story of her
romance with Wild Bill Hickok. At the beginning Calamity (Doris Day) has
an unrequited passion for an army lieutenant, Danny Gilmartin (Phil
Carey), and an ongoing feud with Wild Bill (Howard Keel). Boastfully, she
promises to go to Chicago and bring back to Deadwood the singing star
Adelaid Adams (Gale Robbins), but mistakenly returns with her dresser,
Katie (Allyn McLerie). Katie's impersonation of the star is soon revealed,
but she and Calamity become friends, until Calamity finds out that Katie
and Danny have fallen in love. Calamity draws a gun on Katie, but
having tearfully confessed her sorrows to Wild Bill, Calamity discovers
that he is the one she really loves.

Upon this flimsy structure is constructed a film of great charm and
energy, a great deal of which emanates from Doris Day in the leading
role. She plays the part as a tomboy, innocent of her sexual potential,
determined to out-swagger and out-shoot anyone in the man's world of
Deadwood. With much knee-slapping and an exaggerated western
accent (which disappears when she sings the love songs), she gives a
spirited caricature of the masculinity which is so central to the genre. This
gender-bending theme is pursued elsewhere. Wild Bill, for example, an
uncomplicatedly male figure for most of the film in Howard Keel's rather
static performance, has a bizarre scene in which, in fulfilment of a rash
boast that he would dress up as an Indian squaw should Calamity

succeed in bringing Adelaid Adams to Deadwood, he duly appears in drag cradling a baby. At one point Calamity rescues Danny from Indians, leading Wild Bill to recall later, 'Didn't she save her pretty lieutenant from a fate worse than death?' Though the full implications of this comment are not pursued, mistakes about gender are rife. A visiting actor is forced to go on stage disguised as a woman, while in Chicago, Calamity is twice mistaken for a man, once by a woman in the street who makes eyes at her, and then by Katie.

Calamity's changes of costume map her transition from androgynous buckskin-clad desperado into womanhood, 1950s style. In one extended sequence, as she and Katie clean up her cabin while singing 'A Woman's Touch', Calamity changes to a check shirt and smart pants and then to a pretty lemon-coloured dress. But at the end, singing her big hit 'Secret Love', she is back in Western gear, albeit a much glamorised version of her earlier buckskins.

Dir: David Butler; **Prod**: William Jacobs; **Scr**: James O'Hanlon; **DOP**: Wilfred M. Cline; **Score**: Sammy Fain.

Comanche Station
US, 1960 – 73 mins
Budd Boetticher

This is the last of the films which director Budd Boetticher made in collaboration with Burt Kennedy as screenwriter, Harry Joe Brown as producer and Randolph Scott as star. It follows closely the pattern of the previous ones, with Scott as a laconic, solitary man defeating the odds against him through courage and skill. This time he is Jeff Cody, first discovered riding into Indian country and trading some goods in exchange for a captive white woman, Nancy Lowe (Nancy Gates). Stopping at a stage station on the way back to Lordsburg they see three men approach, pursued by Indians. When the Indians have been fought off, the leader of the newcomers, Ben Lane (Claude Akins), informs Mrs Lowe that there is a $5,000 reward out for her. She thinks less of Cody

Randolph Scott caught out in the open in *Comanche Station*

now she believes that he just rescued her for money. Lane goads Cody and taunts Mrs Lowe with the fact that her husband has not come himself to rescue her. Since the trail is clearly dangerous, the group decide to stick together, but it soon emerges that Lane intends to kill Cody and Mrs Lowe and claim the reward for himself (it has been offered 'dead or alive'). Lane's companions, a couple of amiable drifters, Dobie (Richard Rust) and Frank (Skip Homeier), do not relish killing a woman.

Mrs Lowe's attitude changes when Dobie tells her that Cody has been ten years looking for his wife, who was also captured by Indians. After Cody has offered Dobie help to go straight, Dobie tries to desert Lane, who shoots him in the back. In a final confrontation, Cody gets the drop on Lane, who feels compelled to take a chance ('Got to, come too far to turn back now') and is killed. After discovering that Mrs Lowe's husband is blind, Cody rides off alone, presumably still looking for his wife.

This is a wonderful film, visually elegant, making the most of the harsh landscape of granite rocks and distant mountains near Lone Pine in California. Moments of expertly staged action punctuate quiet scenes by the camp-fire where the battle of wits between Cody and Lane is contested. Akins is another of Boetticher's charming villains: talkative, clever but heartless enough to shoot his friend in the back. Cheerfully amoral in his relations with women, he recounts a troublesome episode with another man's wife, remarking 'Always check the brand to make sure you ain't driving another man's stock.' Scott by contrast is a monument of stoic resilience, spare in his speech but assured in his actions, his face impassive but touched with sadness. Kennedy's dialogue economically delivers insights into the characters. When Dobie asks why Cody is offering him help, Cody simply replies, 'Man gets tired of being all the time alone.' He tells Lane a little parable of a man who came out on top against his opponents, designed to warn Lane off any attempt to kill him. How did he do it, Lane wants to know. 'Let's just say,' Cody answers, 'he had a way with a gun.'

Dir: Budd Boetticher; **Prod**: Harry Joe Brown; **Scr**: Burt Kennedy; **DOP**: Charles Lawton Jr; **Score**: Mischa Bakaleinikoff.

Cowboy
US, 1958 – 92 mins
Delmer Daves

Cowboy has an unlikely source in *My Life and Loves*, the autobiography of the notorious philanderer Frank Harris. His reminiscences of time spent as a cowboy were originally serialised in *Vanity Fair* in 1908, then incorporated into *My Life and Loves* (1922) and later published separately as *On the Trail*. To what extent his tales of cowboy life were authentic is a matter of conjecture. This material was turned into a script by Edward H. North and Dalton Trumbo (who was blacklisted at the time and thus not credited on the screen). The screenwriters leave no trace of the lustful persona that Harris projects in his autobiography, substituting instead a rather earnest character eager for first-hand experience of cowboying and romantically and hopelessly in love. As his protagonist, they build up the character of Reese as a hard-drinking, hard-riding trail boss.

Jack Lemmon would have been strange casting as the real-life Harris, but as the rather gauche young man first discovered as a hotel clerk in Chicago he strikes the right note of awkward charm. Reese (Glenn Ford) and his cowboys come storming into the hotel after a cattle drive up from Texas, demanding hot baths and whisky. Harris has fallen in love with Maria (Anna Kashfi), a Mexican girl staying in the hotel, but her father, a wealthy rancher, intercepts his messages and makes it clear that marriage with his daughter is impossible. Reese gets drunk, loses all his money in a poker game and borrows some from Harris. The next morning, Harris insists that they made a deal for him to become a partner in Reese's enterprise. Greatly to his disgust, Reese is obliged to take the young man with him when they go down to Mexico to buy more cattle. South of the border, Harris renews his acquaintance with Maria, but she has been married off to a local rancher. The resentment

(Opposite page) Trail boss Tom Reese (Glenn Ford) takes a shot at a cockroach in *Cowboy*

between Reese and Harris builds until Reese is shot during an attack by Indians. Harris takes over as trail boss and eventually the two men are reconciled after jointly completing a dangerous task in a moving train.

It's a kind of oedipal narrative, with the younger man challenging the more experienced one, and eventually supplanting him once Reese has suffered his symbolic wounding. Along the way there is an entertaining mix of comedy, adventure and tragedy, of sorts. Reese begins as a larger than life character, sitting in the bath guzzling whisky and shooting at cockroaches on the wall, then dressing up for the opera. He has a nice line in debunking wisdom about cowboy life, warning Harris not to sentimentalise horses ('Did you know that a horse has a brain just about the size of a walnut?') and referring to cattle as 'slab-sided fleabags'. There are stampedes and fights with Indians, and a trail-hand dies after a foolish jape with a rattlesnake. Harris seems determined to become an even harder man than Reese until the two finally bond and achieve mutual respect, Harris having apparently forgotten about his Mexican love.

Dir: Delmer Daves; **Prod**: Julian Blaustein; **Scr**: Edmund H. North, Dalton Trumbo; **DOP**: Charles Lawton Jr; **Score**: George Duning.

Dances With Wolves
US, 1990 – 226 mins
Kevin Costner

In 1990 not many people would have agreed with Kevin Costner that there was still mileage in the traditional Western, after the steep decline in production during the 60s and 70s, and the disasters of the 80s such as *Heaven's Gate*. It is to Costner's credit that he backed his judgment with a story that essentially reworks the traditional captivity narrative. Sent west during the Civil War, Lieutenant John Dunbar (Kevin Costner) finds himself posted to an isolated fort on the plains, apparently deserted by its previous occupants. Gradually he becomes acquainted with a group of Sioux Indians who are camped nearby. As his friendship with them deepens, Dunbar abandons his post and goes native, assisted by a white woman who has lived with the Sioux since childhood. Dunbar and the woman, Stands With a Fist (Mary McDonnell), form a sexual relationship. Dunbar becomes firm friends with Kicking Bird (Graham Greene), assists with a buffalo hunt and helps defend the camp against marauding Pawnees. When Dunbar is captured by the army and charged with desertion, the Sioux rescue him, but eventually Dunbar decides to strike out on his own with Stands With a Fist, fearing that his presence in the Indian camp will only cause the Sioux trouble.

The film is wonderfully photographed, Dean Semler making the most of some breathtaking plains vistas, complemented by John Barry's sweeping score. As the central character, Costner has to shoulder a heavy burden, and if at times his earnestness grates, overall he manages to give the film a high level of sincerity and authenticity. The story is told through the eyes of a white man, and it cannot be denied that what is presented is the kind of Indian that whites prefer: noble, affectionate, humorous, ecologically responsible, in fact an idealised version of ourselves. But in two respects the film represents an important departure. All the Indian roles (and some of them are very substantial) are played by Native American actors; moreover, all the dialogue with

Indians takes place in the Lakota language, with English subtitles. Ironically, this necessitated most of the actors with speaking parts having to learn the language, since only a few of them were Sioux.

Despite these innovations, in some respects Costner can be criticised for timidity. For example, the Sioux appear as a people without fault. As so often in the Western, there are good Indians (quite like us) and bad Indians (the Pawnee), fierce and savage, an implacable Other who must be destroyed. And while in terms of plot it's useful to have a white woman present, since she can interpret for Dunbar before he learns Lakota, to have Dunbar select her instead of a Sioux woman for a sexual partner smacks of compromise with those conventional fears of miscegenation which the Western has suffered from throughout its history. Nevertheless, this is a film of some stature, even more impressive in the director's cut, running nearly four hours.

Dir: Kevin Costner; **Prod**: Kevin Costner, Jim Wilson; **Scr**: Michael Blake; **DOP**: Dean Semler; **Score**: John Barry.

Day of the Outlaw
US, 1959 – 96 mins
André de Toth

The last Western to be directed by the one-eyed Hungarian director
André de Toth, and possibly his best, this has greater intensity than the
series of films he made with Randolph Scott in the early 1950s. Starkly
shot in black and white in a wintry landscape, the story begins with the
bitter fall-out of an illicit romance between local rancher Blaise Starrett
(Robert Ryan) and Helen Crane (Tina Louise), wife of a small farmer. As in
Shane (1953) (both films are set in Wyoming), there is a fierce dispute
between farmers and ranchers over fencing off the land, and Starrett has
threatened to kill Helen's husband if he deploys the barbed wire he has
bought. Just when the quarrel is about to break out into open gunplay,
Jack Bruhn (Burl Ives) bursts in with his outlaw gang. Pursued by soldiers
after committing a robbery, Bruhn's gang seek refuge among the local
townspeople. Bruhn struggles to maintain his authority over his men, a
collection of terrifying cut-throats anxious to get their hands on liquor
and women. In a grotesque scene, Bruhn concedes that they can have a
dance with the women, including Mrs Crane, who are whirled around,
then pawed and molested by the leering outlaws.

Bruhn has a bullet in his chest and although it is removed by the
local vet, he is bleeding to death internally. The problem is, if he dies
before the gang leave, will they wreak a horrifying vengeance? Faced
with such a crisis, Starrett undergoes a transformation. At the
beginning he has been hard, brutal even, delivering a speech very like
that of Ryker in *Shane*, about how the land was nothing when he
found it, and how he had to rid it of 'lice', the undesirable elements,
and thus the land is his by right. 'No pig-bellied farmer is going to stop
me,' he rants. But faced with the threat of Bruhn, he shows his true
mettle, ready by the end to sacrifice himself for the others by leading
Bruhn out into the blizzard in a vain search for an escape trail Starrett
knows is not there.

Up in the mountains, with the snow as high as the horses' bellies, the gang members begin to turn on each other. Then Bruhn dies. Soon there are only two left, with Starrett leading them further and further into the wilderness. Starrett makes an escape, one of the gang is frozen to death overnight and the last one, Tex (Jack Lambert), staggers after Starrett only to collapse in a snowdrift.

It's a tightly knit film with no frills but excellent performances, especially from Ryan, proud, unyielding but ultimately a man of principle, and Ives, ruling his bunch of degenerates with fear and the sheer force of personality. Miraculously, this is one of the few films in which veteran Western actor Elisha Cook, playing the town barber, actually survives to the end.

Dir: André de Toth; **Prod**: Sidney Harmon; **Scr**: Philip Yordan; **DOP**: Russell Harlan; **Score**: Alexander Courage.

Dead Man
US, 1995 – 115 mins
Jim Jarmusch

This takes the Western further down the route of deconstruction than any film since Jean-Luc Godard's *Vent d'est/Wind from the East* (1969). And yet *Dead Man* has its roots deep in the traditional Western, with a story about a greenhorn forced to confront the harsh ways of the frontier. William Blake (Johnny Depp) is an earnest young man from Cleveland coming west by train to the town of Machine, where he has been promised a job as an accountant. As he journeys further away from civilisation, the passengers boarding the train become more and more wild, finally letting off a fusillade of bullets at some passing buffalo. Machine turns out to be a scrofulous little town, with horses pissing in the streets and a whore fellating a customer in broad daylight. Blake registers all this with Depp's customary puzzled air. His prospective employer, Mr Dickinson (Robert Mitchum), chases him away with a gun. Blake is then invited home by Thel (Mili Avital), a young woman he meets in the street, but when her boyfriend Charlie (Gabriel Byrne) turns up and shoots her, Blake kills him in self-defence.

Charlie, it turns out, is Dickinson's son. Now *Dead Man* becomes a tale of revenge and pursuit. Blake is a wanted man, chased by three bounty hunters hired by Dickinson. In the wilderness, he encounters an Indian who calls himself Nobody (Gary Farmer). In the fracas, Blake has himself been shot in the chest and the Indian tries to help him get the bullet out. Nobody proves a kind of New Age Indian, full of mystic sayings and ecological wisdom; at one point he has a vision of Blake as a dead man. Having travelled to England and received an education, Nobody is familiar with the writings of the poet William Blake, and believes the man he has met is one and the same. Meanwhile, Cole Wilson (Lance Henriksen), one of the men pursuing Blake, is reputed to have fucked and eaten both his parents, and soon murders one of his companions, as well as some other men intent on capturing Blake.

There's quite a lot of killing now, as Blake shoots dead two lawmen on his trail. He becomes separated from Nobody, but they meet up again when he surprises Nobody having sex with an Indian girl. Blake is nearly captured by a hypocritical Bible-quoting store-keeper (Alfred Molina) and gets shot once more. Taken to an Indian camp by Nobody, he lapses into a semi-comatose state and is placed in a canoe: 'Time to go back to where you came from,' says Nobody. 'Cleveland?' enquires Blake. 'Back to the place where all the spirits come from,' is the reply.

Shot in glowing black and white by the great Robby Müller and with Neil Young's pounding guitar chords on the soundtrack, this is a strange and original film; not exactly a critique of the Western (for all its squalor and violence), more like a dream, its meandering narrative punctuated by arbitrary and inexplicable events.

Dir: Jim Jarmusch; Prod: Demetra J. MacBride; Scr: Jim Jarmusch; DOP: Robby Müller; Score: Neil Young.

Destry Rides Again
US, 1939 – 94 mins
George Marshall

James Stewart, giving only the faintest hint of the steely inner self he reveals in his later Westerns with Anthony Mann, is the mild-mannered Thomas Jefferson Destry, the son of a famously tough father. The town of Bottleneck is wild and lawless, controlled by crooked gambler Kent (Brian Donlevy) and his accomplice the mayor (Allan Jenkins). Complicit in Kent's schemes to cheat men out of their land and so control the whole valley is Frenchy (Marlene Dietrich), a glamorous singer in the Last Chance saloon. The town drunk, Washington Dimsdale (Charles Winninger), remembers Destry's father and so sends for him to come and clean up the town. But on arrival, Destry is a grave disappointment. Not only is he polite and friendly to all, he doesn't even carry a gun. When he steps off the stage carrying a lady's parasol and a canary in a cage, he immediately becomes an object of ridicule.

One of the film's big set-pieces is a no-holds-barred fight between Frenchy and Lily Belle Callahan (Una Merkel), whose hapless husband Boris (Mischa Auer) has lost his trousers to Frenchy in a poker game. Destry eventually stops the fight by throwing water over the two women, but succeeds only in becoming the new object of Frenchy's wrath as she throw glasses, bottles and chairs at him. Later, however, Destry borrows a hoodlum's gun and demonstrates some fancy shooting, enough to impress the town that he means business.

Kent is a harder nut to crack and Destry knows he will need evidence to convict him. Through a ruse he discovers where Kent has hidden the body of the previous sheriff, whom he has murdered. When Washington is shot by Kent's men Destry finally straps on his gunbelt and goes to the saloon. A battle develops between Kent's lawless followers and the respectable citizens, and Frenchy, who by now has come over to the right side, leads the women of the town into a massed attack on Kent's men. In the ensuing confusion, she throws herself in front of Destry to save him from Kent's bullet (a gesture Dietrich was to repeat in her last Western, *Rancho Notorious* [1952]).

In view of the date when the film was made it's tempting to see it as an allegory about American isolationism before World War II, a policy full of good intentions but untenable given the forces of lawlessness in the world. However, what makes the film so enjoyable, apart from Mischa Auer's hilarious comic turn as a mad Russian, is Stewart's charm and Dietrich's sexual allure. Destry likes to defuse tricky situations with homely stories of people he 'once knew', including most memorably a boy who did in his parents with a crow-bar, then implored the judge to show consideration for the feelings of a poor orphan. Dietrich's singing is, perhaps, an acquired taste, but there's no denying her charisma as, dressed in a glittery Western costume, she belts out 'See what the boys in the backroom will have'.

Dir: George Marshall; **Prod**: Joe Pasternak; **Scr**: Felix Jackson, Henry Myers, Gertrude Purcell; DOP: Hal Mohr; **Score**: Frederick Hollander, Frank Loesser, Frank Skinner.

Django
Italy/Spain, 1966 – 95 mins
Sergio Corbucci

This was a hugely successful film, despite the fact that, because of its excessive violence, it was not originally released in England. Sources differ on the number of sequels it spawned, since many Italian Westerns were subsequently retitled for foreign release to cash in on the *Django* craze. But the number certainly ran into several dozen, including such unlikely titles as *Nude Django*, a sexploitation film from 1971. As Christopher Frayling has shown, the film develops the plot structure first employed in Leone's *A Fistful of Dollars* (1964), with Django, a lone adventurer, pitting himself against rival factions and outwitting them both. When first discovered, Django (Franco Nero) is pulling a coffin behind him as he crosses the border region between the USA and Mexico. He comes across a woman being whipped by Mexican bandits, who are then shot by a group of men wearing red masks (an evocation of the Ku Klux Klan), who propose instead to burn the woman on a cross. But Django intervenes, shooting them all in a dazzling display of virtuosity. Taking the girl, Maria (Loredana Nusciak), to a nearby town, whose only population is a morose saloon-keeper, Nathaniel (Angel Alvarez), and a group of frowsy whores, Django next encounters Major Jackson (Eduardo Fajardo), the leader of the men in red masks, who is still fighting the Civil War, on the side of the Confederates. Producing a heavy machine-gun from his coffin, Django shoots up Jackson's men but saves the Major for special treatment later; apparently the Major was responsible for the death of Django's wife.

The Mexican General Hugo (José Bódalo) now arrives in town and he and Django make friends. Hugo wants to go back to Mexico and fight his enemies, but has no weapons or money. Django says he will sell him machine-guns, and together they steal a sack of gold from Major Jackson's fort. Django then steals the gold for himself and makes off with Maria. But they are chased and the gold is lost in quicksand. The

Mexicans capture Django and break his hands (hence possibly the origins of the hero's name, after the jazz guitarist Django Reinhardt, whose hand was partly disabled). In the final scene, Django lures Jackson to the graveyard, where he manages, despite his mutilation, to fire his pistol.

The fascination with armaments technology was to be a long-standing feature of Italian Westerns, as was anticlericalism, here manifested in a preacher who hypocritically collects money from the brothel for Jackson, then damns the whores. The placing of the action in the Civil War was to return in later films, including Leone's *The Good, the Bad and the Ugly* (1966), the final scene of which also takes place in a graveyard. But the violence of Leone's films is mild compared to *Django*, which besides frequent mass shootings and the prolonged scene in which Django's hands are first beaten with a rifle butt then trampled under horses' hooves, also graphically portrays a man having his ear cut off.

Dir: Sergio Corbucci; **Prod**: Manolo Bolognini; **Scr**: Sergio and Bruno Corbucci, Franco Rossetti, José G. Naesso, Piero Vivarelli; **DOP**: Enzo Barboni; **Score**: Luis Enrique Bacalov.

Dodge City
US, 1939 – 104 mins
Michael Curtiz

A highly successful film in its day, and one of those, together with *Stagecoach* (1939) and *Jesse James* (1939), which helped revive the A-feature Western after the doldrums of the 1930s, *Dodge City* follows the classic pattern of the town-tamer Western. Errol Flynn plays Wade Hatton, a character clearly based on Wyatt Earp who, like Earp in John Ford's *My Darling Clementine* (1946), is at first reluctant to get involved with the problem of lawlessness. But when a small boy whom he has befriended becomes a victim, Hatton accepts the offer to become marshal of Dodge City. The bad elements in the town are controlled by Jeff Surrett (Bruce Cabot), a crooked cattle dealer whose killing is done by Yancey (Victor Jory). With the aid of the local newspaper editor (Frank McHugh), Hatton builds a case against Surrett and has Yancey locked up. He is aided in this by Abbie (Olivia de Havilland), whom he met on the trail from Texas and who takes a job in the newspaper office. When a mob tries to lynch Yancey, Hatton spirits him out of town and onto a train. A fire breaks out and Hatton and his deputies shoot it out with Surrett on the burning train.

Perhaps not surprisingly for a film made in 1939, *Dodge City* is full of nationalistic fervour. After the Civil War, we are told, 'the nation turns to the building of the west'. The train, first seen steaming across the plains towards Dodge City and overtaking a stagecoach, is a symbol of America's future: 'iron men and iron horses – you can't beat 'em.' As so often in the Western, the hero hails from the defeated south. Arriving in town after a cattle drive from Texas, the cowboys Hatton has led up the trail object to a rendering of 'Marching through Georgia' and respond with 'Dixie', leading to the mother of all saloon fights. This spills over into a meeting of the Pure Prairie League, where Hatton's friend Rusty (Alan Hale) is singing hymns in a losing battle against his desire to get rolling drunk; though Hatton favours the respectable people, the devil seems to have the best tunes. Ultimately the west is the place where north and south unite, once the bad elements have been run out of town; it represents the best of America: 'honesty, courage, morality and culture', in the words of one character, though the last seems in short supply. It also stands for cleanliness, Flynn getting a shave while Rusty enjoys 'the only bath-tub between Chicago and Denver'.

Flynn is a personable hero, in an amazingly large hat, though he shows a surprisingly fusty streak when he objects to Abbie working on the paper on the grounds that it's not ladylike. At the end of the picture Colonel Dodge, the head of the railroad and the man after whom the town is named, tells him there's another job of town-taming to be done in Virginia City, Nevada. The next year, 1940, Flynn starred in *Virginia City*, again directed by Michael Curtiz.

Dir: Michael Curtiz; **Prod**: Robert Lord; **Scr**: Robert Buckner; **DOP**: Sol Polito; **Score**: Max Steiner.

Duel in the Sun
US, 1946 – 138 mins
King Vidor

Like *Pursued* (1947), another of Niven Busch's Western family melodramas, the heroine of *Duel in the Sun* is torn between two brothers, one offering a steady but boring respectability, the other danger and romance. *Duel in the Sun* has the added ingredient of racial difference, with Pearl (Jennifer Jones) the daughter of an Indian mother and a white father (Herbert Marshall). When her father is hanged for killing his wife and her lover, Pearl is brought to live with Laura Belle (Lillian Gish), once her father's sweetheart but now married to the crippled and bullying Senator McCanles (Lionel Barrymore), who owns a million acres of Texas. Laura Belle's two sons each fall for Pearl's charms.

A steamy moment from *Duel in the Sun* as Pearl (Jennifer Jones) makes a play for Lewt (Gregory Peck)

Jesse (Joseph Cotten) is studious, a lawyer who treats her with respect. Lewt (Gregory Peck) is a charming but unscrupulous wastrel who wants her as a plaything, an attitude encouraged by his father, who subjects the dark-skinned Pearl to endless racist taunting, calling her squaw and half-breed while demanding: 'How did they come to call you Pearl? Couldn't have had much of an eye for colour.'

When the railroad reaches the edge of his property, the Senator proposes violent resistance, fearing a horde of immigrants will threaten his position. But the army intervenes and he is forced to back down. In his anger he banishes Jesse from the ranch for siding with the legal authorities. The way is now clear for Lewt to have his way with Pearl, and despite being exhorted to virtue by the Sin-Killer (Walter Huston), a charismatic local preacher, she goes swimming with Lewt and later allows him to make love to her during a thunderstorm. But when she demands marriage, Lewt rejects her, and on the rebound she agrees to marry Sam Pierce (Charles Bickford), an older man. In a fit of jealousy Lewt kills him, then goes on the run.

Jesse has become engaged to the daughter of the railroad magnate, but comes back to rescue Pearl when his mother dies. Lewt regards Pearl as his property and shoots Jesse, though he survives. Pearl, fearful that Jesse's friendship for her will endanger his life, goes in search of Lewt. In a finale of extreme emotion, cranked up by Dimitri Tiomkin's swelling music, Pearl tracks Lewt down in the desert and shoots him. But she too is wounded and the two lovers crawl towards each other, their love–hate relationship finally consummated in death.

King Vidor films this torrid tale with a mixture of all-out emotional acting from a starry cast (testing to the limit the abilities of Jennifer Jones, producer David O. Selznick's girlfriend), and striking visual compositions. Figures are outlined in extreme long-shot against the huge skies of Texas, or seen in silhouette before lurid Technicolor sunsets. But underneath the heady melodrama is an archetypal Western conflict between the gun and the law, between wilderness and civilisation and between raw passion and true love, all these opposites finding a home in the heart of poor tormented Pearl.

Selznick spent huge sums on the production and it became a great success at the box office, partly for its (at the time) daring treatment of sex, leading to the film being dubbed 'Lust in the Dust'.

Dir: King Vidor; Prod: David O. Selznick; Scr: David O. Selznick; DOP: Lee Garmes, Harold Rosson, Ray Rennahan; Score: Dimitri Tiomkin.

El Dorado
US, 1966 – 126 mins
Howard Hawks

In adapting Harry Brown's excellent novel *The Stars in Their Courses*, Leigh Brackett essentially reproduced the same characters and situations she had previously written for Howard Hawks in *Rio Bravo* (1959), but with one significant change. To quote from Edgar Allan Poe's poem 'El Dorado', as the character of Mississippi (James Caan) does repeatedly, 'But he grew old, this knight so bold'. Friends from way back, Cole Thornton (John Wayne) and J. P. Harrah (Robert Mitchum), sheriff of El Dorado, have both seen better days. Harrah has become a drunk as the result of an unhappy love affair, while Thornton is carrying a bullet in his back from Joey (Michele Carey), the daughter of Kevin MacDonald (R. G. Armstrong), who is being forced off his ranch by cattle baron Bart Jason (Edward Asner). Thornton, a professional gunfighter, refuses to assist Jason against MacDonald, to whom he feels an obligation, having accidentally shot dead his son (the reason for Joey's attack on him). When Harrah arrests Jason, Thornton joins him in defending the jail against attack, with assistance from the greenhorn Mississippi and cantankerous old-timer Bull Harris (Arthur Hunnicutt).

Thornton resumes an interrupted love affair with Maudie (Charlene Holt), though just like John T. Chance in *Rio Bravo* he has to be chivvied into expressing his true feelings. He also, like Chance, undertakes the rehabilitation of his old friend, bringing him back from alcoholism with a course of tough love which begins with calling a spade a spade: 'I'm looking at a tin star with a drunk pinned on it.' Familiar Hawksian themes are explored, especially the nature of the group bond between fellow professionals, made explicit by Thornton when he remarks, 'This is no job for amateurs.'

(*Opposite page*) Over-egging the pudding: Cole Thornton (John Wayne) about to punch an already comatose J. P. Harrah (Robert Mitchum) in *El Dorado*

There's a lot more humour this time around, with incessant banter about Mississippi's headgear, a strange creation like a sawn-off top hat, given to him by his murdered mentor, and much comical bickering between Harrah and Bull. There's one very funny scene where Harrah has got a flesh wound in the leg and the doctor tells him to stick a finger in the hole while he engages in a lengthy discussion with Thornton about the bullet in his back. Unfortunately Charlene Holt is no Angie Dickinson, and there's a strong sense of déjà vu about some scenes, as when Thornton repeats the trick from the earlier film of tossing a chair through a window to distract his opponents. At the end, having been forced by the kidnapping of one of the MacDonalds to hand over Jason, the four professionals ultimately triumph through a series of ruses involving Mississippi dressing up as a Chinaman and Bull using a bow and arrow. This is unnecessarily convoluted, a poor substitute for the splendid dynamite finale of *Rio Bravo*. But the last scene is wonderfully evocative, as Thornton and Harrah both hobble down the main street on crutches, bloodied but unbowed.

Dir: Howard Hawks; **Prod**: Howard Hawks; **Scr**: Leigh Brackett; **DOP**: Harold Rosson; **Score**: Nelson Riddle.

Face to Face/Faccia a faccia
Italy/Spain, 1967 – 108 mins
Sergio Sollima

In perhaps his most restrained and convincing performance in a spaghetti Western, Gian Maria Volonté plays Brad Fletcher, a Harvard history professor who goes to Texas to convalesce. By chance he encounters outlaw Beauregard Bennett (Thomas Milian), whom he helps escape from the brutal guards who have captured him. In Purgatory City, Beau is offered $5,000 to rid the town of gunmen who are terrorising the citizens. Impressed by Beau's abilities, Brad attaches himself to the outlaw, who now sets about re-forming his gang, known as Beau's Raiders. Brad lectures them on the philosophical underpinnings of morality, while teaching himself to shoot. Beau's men are generally regarded as 'social bandits', targeting corrupt authorities and institutions like banks, but Beau acknowledges that they are essentially anachronisms; 'ghosts of the past', he says, cowboys without cows, prospectors where there is no gold, unable to accept the railroad or the telegraph.

Brad becomes increasingly fascinated with the intellectual challenges of outlawry, and takes over the planning of a bank raid. But his plan comes unstuck, partly because the Raiders have an informer in their midst, Charlie Siringo (William Berger), an historical figure who worked for the Pinkerton Detective Agency. Another factor in the failure of the raid is Beau's refusal to kill a small Mexican boy who runs shouting down the street to give the alarm. As a result, Beau is captured and Brad assumes leadership of the Raiders; as Beau has become soft, so Brad becomes increasingly brutal in his methods. He takes by force a woman he desires, and when her lover fights him, Brad beats him savagely and has to be hauled off; 'I wanted to kill,' he says. By contrast, Beau has refused to exploit Cattle Annie (Carole André), a young and innocent girl who is infatuated with him. When another Pinkerton man is captured, Brad tortures him while lecturing him on the morality of killing: the death of one man is murder, he argues, but 'Violence by masses of men is called history.' Beau escapes from jail, but vigilantes sack the bandits' camp. Brad and Beau lead the survivors out into the desert, where Charlie Siringo catches up with them, and there is a three-way stand-off, in which Brad first wounds Siringo but is himself shot by Beau when he tries to finish him off. Realising that Beau has had enough of killing, Siringo lets him go.

As usual in the Italian Western, there is enough shooting to satisfy those who want action, but the main interest of the film is in the developing relationship between the earnest and serious professor and the charismatic outlaw leader. Brad believes himself to be fully in control of himself, but his intellectualising masks his increasing lust for violence, which provides only a spurious rationale. Christopher Frayling has seen this as a commentary on European Fascism, and given the political climate in which many Italian film-makers worked in the 1960s, it is hard to disagree.

Dir: Sergio Sollima; **Prod**: Alberto Grimaldi; **Scr**: Sergio Sollima; **DOP**: Rafael Pacheco; **Score**: Ennio Morricone.

A Fistful of Dollars/Per un pugno di dollari
Italy/Spain/Germany, 1964 – 97 mins
Sergio Leone

The first of Clint Eastwood's collaborations with Sergio Leone changed not only both their careers, but the history of the Western genre. Until this time known, if at all, for his supporting role in the TV series *Rawhide* (1959–66), Eastwood was cast by Leone for his ability to project a presence on screen without apparently doing anything. As Leone put it:

The Man with No Name (Clint Eastwood) faces up to his responsibilities in *A Fistful of Dollars*

The story is told that when Michelangelo was asked what he had seen in one particular block of marble . . . he replied that he saw Moses. I would offer the same answer to the question, why did I choose Clint Eastwood, only backwards. When they ask me what I saw in Clint Eastwood . . . I reply that what I saw, simply, was a block of marble.

Originally entitled *The Magnificent Stranger*, the plot may owe something to Goldoni's play *The Servant of Two Masters*, and owed a lot more to Kurosawa's 1961 film *Yojimbo*, which occasioned a court case for breach of copyright when Leone's film was released. At the opening a gringo (Eastwood) arrives in a scruffy Mexican town, wearing what became the character's trademark poncho. (In subsequent marketing, the Eastwood character became established as the Man with No Name, though in this first film he is more than once referred to as 'Joe'.) He is informed by the owner of the cantina, Silvanito (José Calvo), that the town is run by two rival gangs, the Baxters and the Rojos. On his way into town the stranger has been insulted by some of the Baxter gang. He now goes to demand an apology and, when it is denied, kills the men in a display of dazzling marksmanship. He offers his services to the Rojo faction and devises a plan to enable them to destroy the Baxters. But things do not work out quite as planned and the stranger falls out with the Rojos, who beat him nearly to death. He escapes, hidden in a coffin by the town undertaker (Josef Egger). The Rojos burn down the Baxters' house and massacre the inhabitants, but the stranger recovers in hiding. In the final sequence he goes up against Ramón Rojo (Gian Maria Volonté) wearing a steel breastplate he has constructed, allowing him to disprove Ramón's earlier assertion that a man with a rifle will always beat a man armed only with a pistol.

The film was a huge international success, leading to the production of several hundred Italian Westerns in the 1960s. Besides Eastwood's undoubted charisma, it benefits from Leone's playful use of Hollywood conventions, spinning out the gunfights with huge close-ups and dramatic use of the wide screen. There is also plenty of laconic humour, as when Eastwood orders three coffins be made ready before his first gunfight, only to revise the order upwards to four at its conclusion. Ennio Morricone's strikingly original music hits the right note from the opening credits, with a whistling motif; like most people on the production, he is credited with a more American-seeming name (Dan Savio).

Dir: Sergio Leone; **Prod**: Arrigo Colombo, Giorgio Papi; **Scr**: Sergio Leone, Duccio Tessari; **DOP**: Massimo Dallamano; **Score**: Ennio Morricone.

For a Few Dollars More/Per qualche dollaro in più
Italy/Spain/Germany, 1965 – 126 mins
Sergio Leone

This is a far better film than the first fruit of the partnership between
Clint Eastwood and Sergio Leone, *A Fistful of Dollars* (1964). It benefits
from a powerful performance from Lee Van Cleef, a veteran of many
Hollywood Westerns, here playing the part of Colonel Mortimer, the
black-clad bounty hunter who forms an uneasy alliance with Monco
(Clint Eastwood). Both are in pursuit of El Indio (Gian Maria Volonté), a
psychopathic bandit who smokes dope and enjoys killing. Having
discovered that El Indio plans to rob the bank in El Paso, Mortimer
suggests that Monco join the gang by breaking one of their number out
of jail. At first suspicious, El Indio is won over by Monco, appreciating the
contrast between his own histrionics and Monco's laidback attitude, as
when Monco laconically remarks that he intends getting an early night:
'If there's gonna be any shooting, I gotta get my rest.'

After El Indio's gang have removed the safe from the El Paso bank,
Mortimer turns up and offers to open it for them. Later he and Monco
steal the money and hide it, but they are set upon by El Indio's men and
savagely beaten. They escape and set about picking off El Indio's men
one by one, assisted by the fact that the bandit has now become
paranoid and is killing his own men. Mortimer and El Indio have a final
confrontation, in which each will fire when a pocket watch in El Indio's
possession stops chiming; the bandit stole the watch from Mortimer's
sister when he raped her (as a result of which she killed herself). Monco
arrives to ensure fair play in this duel; when Mortimer prevails he insists
that Monco take all the rewards for the wanted men, since he has
achieved his revenge.

The film has a much bigger budget than its predecessor and it shows
in the scenes with trains, the frequent changes of location and the
general increase in production values. Morricone's music is even better

than before, and the film has a more assured tone. The rivalry between the two heroes works well, especially in the amusing scene where each competes to shoot up the other's hat. Mortimer boasts an impressive arsenal of weapons, in particular a Buntline model Colt with detachable shoulder-stock. Like Monco, Mortimer has a nice line in sardonic humour, being first discovered on a train reading a Bible, then later goading Wild (Klaus Kinski), one of El Indio's men, before shooting him with a concealed derringer.

Though Mortimer has a personal motive for his quest, Monco, like Joe in the earlier film, is driven only by his lust for money, a characteristic that marks a decisive break with the Hollywood heroic tradition. At the end, totting up the bounty represented by a wagonload of dead bodies, Monco finds his calculations are out, until the last survivor of El Indio's gang appears and Monco can shoot him in order to make his figures add up.

Dir: Sergio Leone; **Prod**: Alberto Grimaldi; **Scr**: Sergio Leone, Luciano Vincenzoni; **DOP**: Massimo Dallamano; **Score**: Ennio Morricone.

Fort Apache
US, 1948 – 127 mins
John Ford

Originally intended to be shot in colour, the first of John Ford's so-called
cavalry trilogy is largely photographed in Monument Valley, which Ford
makes spectacular use of in the action scenes. Based on stories by James
Warner Bellah, *Fort Apache* opposes two rival notions of army life. On
the one hand is Colonel Owen Thursday (Henry Fonda), stiffly formal,
West Point-educated, doing everything by the book. Thursday is ignorant
and contemptuous of the Indians he has been sent to bring under
control. On the other hand is Captain Kirby York (John Wayne), whose
knowledge of Indians comes from experience. Thursday is also a snob,
attempting to prevent the burgeoning relationship between his daughter
Philadelphia (Shirley Temple) and Lieutenant O'Rourke (John Agar), the
son of a mere Sergeant-Major (Ward Bond). Ford's film is full of
affectionate re-creations of the rituals of army life: training in horse-
riding, drill, drinking and dancing, all of which allow for plenty of Ford's
familiar brand of broad comedy, dispensed by Victor McLaglen as the
Irish Sergeant Mulcahy. As always in Ford, dances signify social cohesion
and the celebration of fellowship; those who disrupt them are threats to
the community. Twice Thursday is responsible for breaking up a dance,
thereby alienating himself from all at the fort.

The film is the first of Ford's films to be overtly sympathetic to the
cause of the Indians. The Apache are not the villains; instead, the trouble
has been caused by Meacham (Grant Withers), a rascally Indian agent
whose supplies of liquor Thursday orders destroyed. Thursday despises
his posting to a lonely outpost in the desert but sees an opportunity to
cover himself in glory by bringing the Apache under Cochise to heel.
York is sent out to persuade them to come back over the border from
Mexico, but is then horrified to find that Thursday intends to attack them
with his entire regiment. Disregarding York's advice, Thursday leads his
forces into a trap set by the Apache; they are defeated and Thursday is

killed, a conclusion which is deliberately intended to evoke the foolhardy actions of General Custer at the Battle of the Little Big Horn. In an intriguing coda, York is playing host to a group of newspapermen after the disaster. They discuss a painting of Thursday leading the charge, and York deliberately conceals his knowledge of what actually happened, alleging that 'No man died more gallantly. Nor won more honour for his regiment.' Ostensibly Ford seems to be saying, as apparently he says in *The Man Who Shot Liberty Valance* (1962), that the country needs its myths, even if they are based on falsehood. But since we, the audience, have already seen the shameful result of Thursday's arrogance, the effect of the film, far from preserving the myth, is to eat away at its foundations. York is merely saving the army's face.

Dir: John Ford; Prod: John Ford, Merian C. Cooper; Scr: Frank S. Nugent; DOP: Archie Stout; Score: Richard Hageman.

Forty Guns
US, 1957 – 80 mins
Samuel Fuller

A town-taming Western which has something in common with the
Wyatt Earp story, *Forty Guns* is also a prime example of the mature style
of Sam Fuller. Barbara Stanwyck is the imperious Jessica Drummond, a
ranch-owner who gallops around on a white horse, with her forty
retainers in tow and accompanied by a theme song: 'She's a high-riding
woman with a whip'. When her younger brother Brockie (John Ericson) is
arrested for the malicious shooting of the town sheriff, Jessica, dressed in
tight-fitting black jeans and shirt and carrying a whip, strides into the jail
and demands his release. Griff Bonnell (Barry Sullivan) is passing through,
on the trail of a fugitive, but when his brother Wes (Gene Barry) takes a
shine to Louvenia (Eve Brent), a young woman who makes guns ('I never
kissed a gunsmith before'), Griff decides to stay. Jessica has the county
marshal Ned Logan (Dean Jagger) in her pay, but, immediately taken
with Griff, she offers him the job instead. Griff is starting to weary of his
profession as a law enforcer, telling his young brother Chico (Robert Dix)
that he is a freak, out of his time, and that a new era is coming. Jessica
offers him a way out, reinforcing the point: 'This is the last stop, Griff.
The frontier is finished.' But Griff does not want to be one of her
minions. Griff survives an attempt by Brockie to have him killed, and
Logan also takes a shot at him. Jessica explains that the motive is
jealousy, and when she spurns Logan's offer of love he hangs himself.
The feud between Brockie and the Bonnells takes a dramatic turn when
Wes is shot and killed at his wedding to Louvenia. Griff arrests Brockie,
and once more Jessica goes to the jail. But this time she is dressed in
feminine clothes, and tells Brockie he must take his medicine. Brockie
busts out of jail, using his sister as a shield, but Griff confronts him, first
shooting Jessica and then killing Brockie. Jessica survives, since Griff has
only shot to wound her, and as he rides away Jessica swallows her pride
and runs after him.

Fuller's cinema is brash, even vulgar, but its raw power is undeniable. *Forty Guns* is full of stunning moments: Jessica's first eruption onto the scene, the shooting at the wedding, Logan's suicide and, most memorably, the daring of the scene in which Griff shoots through Jessica in order to get at Brockie. To communicate Fuller's vision of life as an elemental struggle between egos, the dialogue does not fight shy of melodrama; as Jessica kisses Griff she tells him, "What's happened between us is like a war, easy to start and hard to stop.' Sexual desire and violence are never far apart, whether it's Wes eyeing Louvenia through the barrel of a Winchester before telling Griff, 'I'd like to stay around long enough to clean a rifle,' or Jessica asking Griff if she can feel his gun.

Dir: Samuel Fuller; **Prod**: Samuel Fuller; **Scr**: Samuel Fuller; **DOP**: Joseph Biroc; **Score**: Harry Sukman.

The Good, the Bad and the Ugly/
Il buono, il brutto, il cattivo
Italy/USA, 1966 – 154 mins
Sergio Leone

This is the last and the most ambitious of Sergio Leone's three films with Clint Eastwood. To the rivalry between the Eastwood character (here called Blondie) and the Lee Van Cleef character (here called Angel Eyes) Leone has added a third ingredient, that of Eli Wallach, playing Tuco. These three are, respectively, the good, the bad and the ugly, though Blondie's virtue lies merely in not being quite as unscrupulous as the other two. As in the two previous outings, he remains motivated only by money. Not for Leone the high-minded aims of Hollywood Western heroes, to impose civilisation on the wilderness or make the town safe for women and children.

Blondie and Tuco are first introduced operating a neat little scam in which Blondie captures Tuco, delivers him to the authorities in exchange for the reward, then sets him free again just as he is about to be hanged. Blondie grows weary of the game and leaves Tuco stranded, but Tuco returns, steals a gun from a gunsmith and forces Blondie out into the desert. There, improbably, they come upon a coach in which a dying man tells Tuco the name of the cemetery in which he has hidden $200,000. But only Blondie gets to hear the name on the grave which hides the loot.

Blondie and Tuco find themselves in the middle of the Civil War, are captured by Union troops and imprisoned. Angel Eyes is also in pursuit of the money and turns up as one of their jailers. He tortures Tuco into telling him where the cemetery is, then takes Blondie with him to dig up the money. After a series of incidents in which first one, then the other, has the upper hand, all three of them arrive at the cemetery and there is

(*Opposite page*) Finally Blondie (Clint Eastwood) has Tuco (Eli Wallach) just where he wants him in *The Good, the Bad and the Ugly*

a three-way face-off. Angel Eyes is shot and though Blondie spares Tuco, he leaves him stranded once more.

The film is on an impressive scale, with an epic battlefield sequence like something out of World War I, which concludes with the spectacular blowing up of a bridge. 'I've never seen so many men wasted so badly,' says Blondie in philosophical mood. The scenes in the prison camp are unusually sombre for a Leone film. As Tuco is beaten within an inch of his life, Angel Eyes orders the camp orchestra to play. 'More feeling,' snarls one of the guards at the violinist; the reference to the orchestras assembled in the Nazi death camps is inescapable.

However, what one chiefly finds in the film is an infectious sense of fun. Tuco as played by Wallach is an inspired creation, sly and devious, revelling in his own malevolent schemes. At one of the hangings from which Blondie rescues him, a seemingly endless list of his crimes is read out, and one believes he may well have committed them all, such is his appetite for wickedness. Eastwood looks on with an amused smile, as if scarcely able to believe the cunning with which the picture is being stolen from him.

Dir: Sergio Leone; **Prod**: Alberto Grimaldi; **Scr**: Age Scarpelli, Luciano Vincenzoni, Sergio Leone; **DOP**: Tonino Delli Colli; **Score**: Ennio Morricone.

Go West
US, 1925 – 69 mins
Buster Keaton

Despondent at his inability to find a job in rural Indiana, 'Friendless', as Buster Keaton is named in this film, travels to the big city, but is literally overwhelmed by the crowds and trampled underfoot. He has a vision of Horace Greeley, the journalist, exhorting him to 'Go west, young man,' and hops on a Santa Fe freight train. Deposited in the wide open spaces of the south-west, he grabs a discarded pair of chaps and tries to imitate the swaggering walk of a cowboy. His first job on a ranch is to milk a cow, a scene of wondrous Keatonian comedy. Friendless soon forms a close relationship with the cow, dubbed Blue Eyes, which inadvertently saves him from a mauling by a bull. Forbidden to bring his new friend into the bunk-house, Friendless takes to sleeping in the cow-shed, and when Blue Eyes is threatened with being branded, he applies shaving cream to her rump and carefully shaves on a brand to spare her suffering.

Western comedies usually have fun at the expense of the macho world of the frontier, and this is no exception. Friendless is no coward, but he is tender-hearted. When the rancher decides to send his cattle to the slaughter-house, Friendless tries to buy Blue Eyes to save her, but he has no money. He gets in a card game, hoping to win some, but feels obliged to point out that his opponent is cheating. 'When you say that, smile,' says the man with an evil leer, echoing the famous phrase from Owen Wister's influential novel, *The Virginian*. Friendless's response is to draw a tiny little pistol he has found earlier in a lady's handbag, but the gesture does not impress.

Friendless gets on the train carrying Blue Eyes and the other cattle to the stockyards, and when it is attacked by another rancher who wants to hold out for high prices, Friendless suddenly finds himself on the runaway train as it careers headlong towards Los Angeles. Miraculously slowing the train just as it reaches the buffers, Friendless buys a ticket to put Blue Eyes in a car park while he attempts to round up the hundreds of cattle that have escaped from the train. A full-scale riot ensues as the cattle invade barber shops and women's clothing stores, causing mass panic. Remembering that waving something red at a steer will attract its attention, Friendless improbably dresses himself in a scarlet devil's costume, running through the streets just ahead of the rampaging cattle until they are safely corralled at the stockyards. The grateful rancher offers him anything he wants in reward. The rancher's daughter looks at him with a simper, but Friendless chooses Blue Eyes.

A wonderfully fresh and innocent film, performed and directed with all Keaton's deftness and grace, *Go West* is accompanied on the Kino DVD by *The Paleface* (1921), a short in which Buster is a butterfly collector who strays into an Indian camp, is adopted by the tribe and helps them save their reservation from crooked land grabbers.

Dir: Buster Keaton; **Prod**: Buster Keaton; **Scr**: Raymond Cannon; **DOP**: Bert Haines, Elgin Lessley.

Great Day in the Morning
US, 1956 – 92 mins
Jacques Tourneur

This is the last Western to be directed by Jacques Tourneur, and probably the best. It's set in Colorado just before the start of the Civil War. In Denver, opposing factions of north and south are sparring, jockeying for advantage in an atmosphere of suspicion and hysteria. Out on the trail, Owen Pentecost (Robert Stack) meets Ann (Virginia Mayo) and strikes up an acquaintanceship, as well as encountering Zeph Masterson (Leo Gordon), a rabidly pro-Northern supporter who, discovering Pentecost's southern origins threatens him. In Denver, Pentecost gets into a poker game with Jumbo Means (Raymond Burr), the owner of the Circus Tent saloon. Having lost all his money, Jumbo bets his property on a single turn of the cards. Saloon girl Boston (Ruth Roman), who hates Jumbo, cheats so that Pentecost wins and acquires the saloon. Pentecost then gets drunk and makes advances to Ann; Boston leads him away but he falls asleep before she can make love to him.

Though a southerner, Pentecost professes to be interested in nothing but money. He offers a group of southern miners the use of wagons and supplies so they can transport their gold to the south to pay for weapons for the Confederacy, but only in exchange for a share. Having acquired some mining claims along with the saloon, Pentecost offers to stake anyone to work the claims if they will share fifty-fifty. But, riding out with Ann one day, he discovers a miner is cheating him. In a gun duel, Pentecost kills the man. Later he decides to be a foster parent to the man's son, Gary, without telling the boy he killed his father. Caught between the two women vying for his affections, and between the increasingly aggressive factions of north and south, wracked by his guilty secret concerning the boy, Pentecost maintains his air of insouciance with increasing difficulty. When he is wounded in a fracas, Boston accuses Ann of wanting to change him, while she is prepared to accept him as he is.

Having given Gary shooting lessons ('No gun is a toy'), much to
Ann's disgust, Pentecost eventually discloses he has killed the boy's
father. Gary picks up a gun to shoot him but cannot do so. In a furious
finale, Boston is murdered by Jumbo, who is in turn killed in a fight
between north and south, and Pentecost helps the southern miners
escape. Captured by an army officer who is his rival for Ann, Pentecost
convinces him that Boston was the one he truly loved and is allowed to
go free.

This highly melodramatic tale is enriched not only by Tourneur's
intelligent and sensitive *mise en scène*, but by the complex
characterisation of the hero. Pentecost is oddly passive in Stack's
personification, watching with his trademark smirk as the two women,
the contrast in their characters highlighted by the blonde/brunette
dichotomy, vie for his attention. He is likewise disdainful of the passions
that animate the political factions. Only for the boy whom he has
orphaned does he feel any genuine love, and he knows that this may not
survive the disclosure of his role in his father's death.

Dir: Jacques Tourneur; **Prod**: Edmund Grainger; **Scr**: Lesser Samuels; **DOP**: William Snyder;
Score: Leith Stevens.

The Great K & A Train Robbery
US, 1926 – 53 mins
Lewis Seiler

Tom Mix was the greatest of all the Western stars of the silent era. First discovered working for the Miller Brothers 101 Ranch Wild West Show, he appeared in *Ranch Life in the Great Southwest*, a Selig film from 1910. Further film roles followed, but it was not until Mix joined Fox in 1917 that his career took off, in a series of fast-moving action-packed entertainments which showcased the star's abilities as a rider. In contrast to William S. Hart, the other major star of the period, Mix was flamboyant and fun-loving, appearing in a succession of flashy costumes and emphasising the romantic, fantasy side of Western life, not the downbeat realism preferred by Hart. Whereas Hart's roots were in the legitimate stage, Mix never lost touch with the world of rodeo and wild west shows, and periodically returned to live performance.

By the mid-1920s, he was starring in six or seven films a year and earning $17,000 a week from the studio, with additional revenues from advertising breakfast cereals and other products. Attempts by the studio to broaden his appeal by putting him in costume films such as *Dick Turpin* (1925) outraged his fans and Fox quickly reverted to the Western formula. *The Great K & A Train Robbery* is typical of his films from this period, opening with a spectacular stunt as Tom slides down from a cliff on a cable, right onto the back of his horse, Tony. Riding off in pursuit of a girl in a runaway buggy, he rescues her just before it turns over. She proves to be Madge (Dorothy Dwan), the daughter of the president of the K & A railroad (William Walling), which Tom is defending against the depredations of bandits. The president's male secretary Burton Holt (Carl Miller) is wooing the girl, but he's a cissy ('If he went to college it was Vassar!') and no match for the virile Tom when he discovers that the secretary is selling railroad secrets to the bandits.

Like the singing cowboys of the following decade, Mix inhabits a world recognisably Western in its iconography (six-guns, horses and so forth), but at the same time contemporary. Tom gets assistance from a whiskery tramp (Harry Grippe), who proves to have been with Tom at the battle of Verdun in World War I. (The largely fictional biography constructed by the studio for the star invented several episodes of service in the military, including enlistment with Teddy Roosevelt's Rough Riders, fighting in the Philippines and against the British in the Boer War.)

The riding stunts at least are genuine and are mostly performed by Mix himself. Having rescued the girl from the buggy, he rides up alongside a moving train and carefully deposits her on the caboose. At the end of the film Tom engages in an epic fistfight with the entire bandit gang, emerging bedraggled but triumphant. But by 1930, Mix was fifty years old and his film career was nearly over. He died in a car crash in 1940.

Dir: Lewis Seiler; **Prod**: Lewis Seiler; **Scr**: John Stone; **DOP**: Dan Clark.

The Great Train Robbery
US, 1903 – 12 mins
Edwin S. Porter

Most histories claim *The Great Train Robbery* as the first Western,
initiating a genre that was in a few short years to become the most
popular in American cinema. Made by the Edison Company in November
1903, *The Great Train Robbery* was the most commercially successful film
of the pre-Griffith period of American cinema and spawned a host of
imitations.

What is exceptional about Porter's film is the degree of narrative
sophistication, given the early date. There are over a dozen separate
scenes, each one developing the story. In the opening scene, two
masked robbers force a telegraph operator to send a false message so
that the train will make an unscheduled stop. In the next scene, bandits
board the train. In scene three, the robbers enter the mail car and after a
fight, open the safe. In the next scene, two robbers overpower the driver
and fireman of the train and throw one of them off. Next, the robbers
stop the train and hold up the passengers. One runs away and is shot.
Then the robbers escape aboard the engine and in the subsequent scene
we see them mount horses and ride off. Meanwhile the telegraph
operator on the train sends a message calling for assistance. In a saloon,
a tenderfoot is being forced to dance at the point of a gun, but when
the message arrives, everyone grabs their rifles and exits. Cut to the
robbers pursued by a posse. There is a shootout and the robbers are
killed.

There's one extra shot, the best known in the film, showing one of
the robbers firing point blank out of the screen. This was, it seems,
sometimes shown at the start of the film, sometimes at the end. Either
way, it gave the spectator a sense of being directly in the line of fire.

One of the actors in the film was G. M. Anderson (real name Max
Aronson). Among other parts, he played the passenger who is shot.
Anderson was to shortly become the first actor to become a star of

The famous 'in your face' shot which concludes the first Western ever made, *The Great Train Robbery*

Westerns, appearing as Broncho Billy in over 100 films from 1907.

In later years some have challenged the claim of *The Great Train Robbery* to be regarded as the first Western, on the grounds either that it is not the first, or that it is not a Western. It is certainly true that there are earlier films with a Western theme, such as Edison's *Cripple Creek Bar-room* (1899), but they do not have the fully developed narrative of Porter's film. It's also true that it has antecedents in stage plays incorporating spectacular railroad scenes, and in other films of daring robberies which weren't Westerns. Nor can its claim to being a true Western be based on authentic locations, since *The Great Train Robbery* was shot on the Delaware and Lackawanna Railroad in New Jersey. But train robberies had since the days of Jesse James been part of Western lore, and other iconic elements such as six-shooters, cowboy hats and horses give the film a genuine Western feel.

Dir: Edwin S. Porter; **Scr**: Edwin S. Porter; **DOP**: Edwin S. Porter.

The Grey Fox
Canada, 1982 – 91 mins
Phillip Borsos

It's 1901. After thirty-three years in San Quentin, ageing outlaw Bill
Miner (Richard Farnsworth) is released into a world that has moved on.
On a train, a salesman demonstrates the latest household gadgets to
Bill's bemusement. Bill's speciality has been robbing stagecoaches, but
now there are none left to rob. Moving up to Canada, he finds work
gathering oysters, but his heart is not in it. He thinks about becoming a
goldminer, but is informed the gold rush is over. 'Seems like I missed out
on all the good opportunities,' says Bill with regret. Inspired by watching
The Great Train Robbery (1903) at the movies, and armed with a newly
purchased Colt revolver, he and some other men hold up a train, but
their incompetence leads to one of the gang being captured and he
gives Bill's name to the police. On the run, Bill acquires another partner
in crime, Shorty (Wayne Robson), and together they rob a train, this time
successfully. Hiding out under an assumed name, Bill begins a
relationship with Kate (Jackie Burroughs), a feminist photographer,
though Bill tells her he is superstitious about having his picture taken.
The Pinkertons are on his trail and from the description being circulated,
Kate recognises that Bill is a wanted man. She agrees to meet him later
after he has given the authorities the slip, but after another robbery goes
wrong, Shorty is shot and both of them are arrested. Bill is given twenty-
five years in jail. However, a title informs us, in 1907 Bill escaped and
was never heard of again.

A surprisingly tender film for a Western, *The Grey Fox*, a Canadian
production, is full of affection for its game if ageing protagonist. Bill is
marvellously played by Farnsworth, a veteran of many Westerns who
achieved this starring role late in life. Clad in woolly jumpers and a
battered old hat, Bill makes an unlikely hero, but Farnsworth's sad,
gentle face illuminates the screen. The film also has some agreeably
quirky moments, as when Bill comes across Kate in the woods, belting

golf balls into the trees to the accompaniment of grand opera on a phonograph. There's a suggestion that Bill becomes a folk hero à la Jesse James on account of only robbing the railroads, not individuals, but the film wisely does not attempt to overload its story with significance, preferring to work in a minor key with humour and irony. Shorty too is an engaging character. Bill reads to him a newspaper account of themselves, in which Shorty is described as 'short, dirty, nervous and unintelligent'. 'Hell, I've never been nervous in my life,' is his sole response. With wistful Irish music by the Chieftains, this is a film strong on character and atmosphere, with a lovely period feel and a delightfully upbeat ending as Bill, clad in prison uniform, steals a boat and rows away into the mist.

Dir: Phillip Borsos; Prod: Peter O'Brian; Scr: John Hunter; DOP: Frank Tidy; Score: Michael Conway.

Gunfight at the O.K. Corral
US, 1956 – 122 mins
John Sturges

Not the first version of the Wyatt Earp story, nor the latest, and no more an accurate account of historical events than any of the others, *Gunfight at the O.K. Corral* benefits from powerful performances from its two stars, Burt Lancaster as Earp and Kirk Douglas as Doc Holliday. The film opens in a very downbeat manner in the town of Griffin, showing us the

On their way to meet the Clantons at the O.K. Corral: Doc Holliday (Kirk Douglas), Wyatt Earp (Burt Lancaster), Virgil Earp (John Hudson) and Morgan Earp (DeForest Kelley)

degrading relationship between Holliday and Kate Fisher (Jo Van Fleet), each despising the other almost as much as themselves ('You're dirt. Just like me,' says Kate). When Holliday is forced to confront the menacing Bailey (Lee Van Cleef), Wyatt helpfully informs him of the derringer Bailey keeps in his boot, but Holliday is reluctant to become friends with a lawman. Back in Dodge City, where Earp is marshal, Doc is permitted by Earp to remain only on condition he keeps his nose clean: 'no knives, no guns, no killings'. When Kate takes up with Johnny Ringo (John Ireland), Doc refuses to fight him, even though provoked, because he has given Earp his word, and when cattle baron Shanghai Pierce (Ted de Corsia) hits town with his cowboys, Doc backs up Earp in the ensuing fight. Now firm friends, the pair move on to Tombstone, where Wyatt's brother James is killed by the Clanton clan. Wyatt tries to defuse the situation by counselling the drunken young Billy Clanton (Dennis Hopper) but a final confrontation becomes inevitable. Doc, his TB now at an advanced stage, discovers Kate is helping the Clantons against the Earps and is about to kill her when he collapses. He drags himself up off his sick-bed to join the Earps at the O.K. Corral, where they settle their scores against the Clanton gang.

Among the inventions of the film is a love affair for Wyatt with Laura Denbow (Rhonda Fleming), a lady gambler whom he initially arrests but then pursues. Like Virgil's wife, Laura wants Wyatt to abandon the law for a safer career, but his honour and his family exert the stronger pull; together with, of course, his friendship with Holliday, a prime example of the male bonding so dear to the heart of the genre. Wyatt and Doc are opposites who attract: the former stiffly upright (Doc calls him 'Preacher'), morally unbending but immense in his strength and authority, the latter reckless with his health and self-respect in the pursuit of pleasure.

Sturges' direction is assured, especially in the slickly choreographed action sequences, and though the film mainly takes places in smoke-filled saloons and dingy hotel rooms, there's an appropriate bleakness about the wintry landscapes, shot in the wide-screen process of VistaVision.

Frankie Laine's singing of the theme song helped to make the film a big hit, but it's Kirk Douglas's performance that sticks in the mind, whether swigging down aftershave in the barber shop or sitting down at the poker table after all the killing with the sprightly question, 'What's the name of this game?' Some critics rate Sturges' 1967 sequel, *Hour of the Gun*, with James Garner as Wyatt, an even better film.

Dir: John Sturges; **Prod**: Hal B. Wallis; **Scr**: Leon Uris; **DOP**: Charles B. Lang; **Score**: Dimitri Tiomkin.

The Gunfighter
US, 1950 – 84 mins
Henry King

The theme of the world-weary gunfighter who has outlived his time and wants to settle down came to be a familiar one in the decades after this film, but it was still fresh in 1950. Gregory Peck is Jimmy Ringo, perhaps 'the fastest man with a gun who ever lived', as the opening titles speculate. His reputation attracts those wanting to make a name for themselves, and when one of them (Richard Jaeckel) draws on him, Jimmy shoots him dead. He leaves town with the man's three brothers in hot pursuit. Arriving in Cayenne he encounters his old friend Mark (Millard Mitchell), who though once a badman is now marshal. Jimmy implores him to tell his former girlfriend Peggy (Helen Westcott), now a schoolteacher living in town under an assumed name, that he wants to see her. But she refuses to meet him. Jimmy knows that his pursuers are only an hour or two behind, but encountering another old friend, Molly (Jean Parker), he persuades her to bring Peggy to him. Meanwhile Hunt Bromley (Skip Homeier), another boastful young man looking to become famous, tries to provoke Jimmy into a fight but fails. 'Seems to me there's a squirt like you in every town in the west,' Jimmy remarks scornfully. Jimmy tries to persuade Peggy that he is tired of his old life and wants to settle down ('Here I am, thirty-five years old and I ain't even got a good watch'), but she is unconvinced. At last the three pursuers arrive, but they are prevented from shooting Jimmy by the law. Just as Jimmy is about to leave town, having secured Peggy's promise to see him again in a year's time, Hunt emerges from hiding and shoots him dead.

Yet another film from the 50s which relies on the tension of time ticking by (as in *High Noon* [1952] and *3.10 to Yuma* [1957]), *The Gunfighter* is nicely paced, mixing shots of the avenging brothers drawing closer with the gradual revelation of Jimmy's past life, and the frequently humorous depiction of a small town brought to life by the presence of notoriety. At the barber's shop the card-players decline to risk danger watching Hunt show off ('I've got a mother who's my sole supporter,' says one). In the marshal's office the town busybodies demand that action be taken to expel the murderous Ringo, unaware that they are standing right in front of him. Millard Mitchell gives splendid support as the older and wiser marshal, and Karl Malden is marvellously unctuous as the bartender anxious to bask in Jimmy's reflected glory. But it is Peck's film, tender with his young hero-worshipping son, nerveless as he bluffs Hunt about having a gun on him under the table, and at the end witheringly contemptuous as, mortally wounded, he curses Hunt, not wanting him to hang but instead to live in fear of being himself shot by a glory-hunter: 'I want you to see what it means to live like a big tough gun.'

Dir: Henry King; **Prod**: Nunnally Johnson; **Scr**: William Bowers, William Sellers; **DOP**: Arthur Miller; **Score**: Alfred Newman.

The Hanging Tree
US, 1959 – 106 mins
Delmer Daves

'To really live you must almost die,' says a character at the end of *The Hanging Tree*. Dr Joseph Frail is a man only half alive at the beginning of the film, oppressed by some secret tragedy in his past. He takes a house in a goldmining camp (it is Montana in the 1870s), then saves the life of Rune, a young boy caught stealing, and tends his wounds on condition the boy becomes his bonded servant. Frail's status as a doctor is challenged by Grubb (George C. Scott), a half-crazed religious healer. Out in the wilds a stagecoach is attacked; thrown from the wreckage is Elizabeth Mahler (Maria Schell) a young woman from Switzerland. When she is found by Frenchy (Karl Malden), a miner, she has been blinded by exposure to the sun. Doc Frail nurses her back to health; fiercely protective, he gives Frenchy a beating when he molests Elizabeth. But when she gets her sight back, Doc's attitude to her hardens; he cannot bring himself to admit his feelings. Refusing to go back to Switzerland, Elizabeth decides to go into partnership with Frenchy; unknown to her Doc arranges for her to get credit at the store. When she discovers the truth, Elizabeth accuses him of cruelty in drawing people to him, then turning them away. At last Doc reveals his secret; his wife had killed herself after an affair with his brother; Doc had burned their house to the ground.

A 'glory hole' is discovered on Elizabeth's claim (under a fallen tree a rich hoard of nuggets is found in the roots) and the town gets drunk. While Grubb whips the mob into a frenzy, turning them against Doc, Frenchy tries to rape Elizabeth. Doc shoots Frenchy and throws his body over a cliff. The mob seize Doc and drag him to the hanging tree ('every mining camp's got to have its hanging tree, makes folks feel respectable', a character remarks early on). Elizabeth offers all her gold to the mob in return for sparing Doc. At last he can learn to live again.

As always in the Western, gold brings nothing but trouble, dangerous passions constantly erupting. Doc's house is on the edge of a precipitous cliff and the dizzying crane shots of director Daves emphasise its symbolic significance for Doc, maintaining his aloofness far above the ordinary mass as the only way of keeping a lid on his emotions. His iron self-control contrasts with the unbridled passion of the hate-filled Grubb and the lustful Frenchy, but he is a man frozen into himself to the point where his emotional restraint is a form of cruelty. 'Do you like to torture?' an anguished Elizabeth asks him. Gary Cooper is perfect for the role, his lined face evocative of his suffering even though he will admit nothing. By contrast, Maria Schell, fresh from her role in Visconti's *Le notti bianche/White Nights* (1957), is affecting as the woman who, having been brought back to life by Doc, rescues him from a living death.

Dir: Delmer Daves; **Prod**: Martin Jurow, Richard Shepherd; **Scr**: Wendell Mayes, Halsted Welles; **DOP**: Ted McCord; **Score**: Max Steiner.

Heaven's Gate
US, 1980 – 219 mins
Michael Cimino

The film is broadly based on the events of the Johnson County War in
Wyoming in the early 1890s, in which the Wyoming Stock Growers'
Association hired a party of gunmen to attack immigrant settlers, whom
they believed were rustling their cattle. In Michael Cimino's film, Jim
Averill (Kris Kristofferson) is a wealthy man who takes the side of the
poor immigrants against Frank Canton (Sam Waterston), the leader of
the cattlemen. Jim and Nate Champion (Christopher Walken) are rivals
for the affections of Ella Watson (Isabelle Huppert), a local prostitute.
(Both Nate and Ella were historical characters who figured in the events
in Johnson County.) The Stock Growers have produced a list of 125
people they intend to execute; Ella is on the list because she accepts
stolen cattle as payment. At first Nate is on the side of the cattlemen,
but his love for Ella sees him increasingly antagonistic to them. He offers
to marry Ella and take her away, but she finds it hard to choose between
the two men. Then Ella's brothel is attacked by the hired gunmen and
she is brutally raped, though rescued by Jim. When Nate breaks with the
cattlemen, he becomes a victim, his cabin surrounded and set on fire.
Ella finds his bullet-riddled body. A mob of settlers now ride out against
the gunmen and besiege them. A bloody fight ensues, in which under
Jim's direction, the settlers launch fortified wagons against their
adversaries. Before the settlers can kill all the gunmen, the army arrives
to rescue them. Jim and Ella prepare to go away, but Canton ambushes
them and Ella is killed. In an epilogue set in 1903, Jim cruises on his
yacht with his prim but elegant wife.

  Heaven's Gate has become notorious in the annals of Hollywood
both for the extravagance of its production and for its disastrous
showing at the box office, which put the dampers on the further
production of Westerns for a decade. The story is told in all its lurid detail
in *Final Cut*, a memoir by Steve Bach, who was an executive of United

Artists at the time the film was made. However, in the years since the debacle of its release the film has been critically rehabilitated, in part because a director's cut, now running at a lengthy 219 minutes, allows the full sweep of Cimino's vision to be appreciated. Rarely for a big-budget Hollywood film, the role of class in American society is fully explored. The immigrants are dirt-poor, Russian- or German-speaking, reduced to dragging their ploughs by hand, and unsophisticated, even brutish, in their pleasures, such as cock-fighting. By contrast, the rich are impeccably dressed and utterly callous. Jim's friend John Bridges (Jeff Bridges) remarks, 'It's getting to be dangerous to be poor in this country.' 'It always was,' retorts Jim. This is the west of the New Western History, stripped of the myths of progress and Manifest Destiny, with capitalism running roughshod over its victims, albeit against the splendour of the Wyoming Rockies.

Dir: Michael Cimino; **Prod**: Joann Carelli; **Scr**: Michael Cimino; **DOP**: Vilmos Zsigmond; **Score**: David Mansfield.

Heller in Pink Tights
US, 1960 – 100 mins
George Cukor

From Louis L'Amour's tediously conventional novel, director George Cukor fashioned a thing of grace and beauty. With a script by Walter Bernstein and Dudley Nichols (who wrote *Stagecoach* [1939]), the film recounts the Wyoming adventures of a troupe of travelling actors under the leadership of Tom Healy (Anthony Quinn). The company includes Angie Rossini (Sophia Loren), with whom Healy has an on-off relationship, Mrs Hathaway (Eileen Heckart), a lady of a certain age, her soubrette daughter Della (Margaret O'Brien) and the ageing Doc Montagu (Edmund Lowe). Perpetually on the run from creditors, Healy thinks they have finally got it made in Cheyenne, where Angie's performance in 'Mazeppa', bound in flesh-coloured tights to a galloping horse, is a sensation. But Angie loses when she bets herself in a poker game with professional gunman Mabry (Steve Forrest), and Healy insists they do a moonlight flit before Mabry can collect. Mabry follows and rescues them from Indian attack, but Healy is mistakenly shot in the leg by an assassin sent by De Leon (Ramon Novarro), who would prefer not to pay Mabry for the numerous killings he has had him carry out. While Healy recovers at a mission, Angie attempts reconciliation but Healy is cold; when she protests that her bet with Mabry was only a game, he curtly replies, 'I'm too old for games.' Angie goes on alone to Bonanza, where she collects the money De Leon owes Mabry but spends it on buying a theatre for Healy. When at last Mabry comes to collect, Healy finds an ingenious way for him to escape De Leon, and thus the debt is finally paid.

Anthony Quinn is marvellous as the long-suffering Healy, still carrying a torch for Angie despite all her deceptions. A man dedicated to his art, however tawdry, and the complete opposite of the crudely macho Mabry, he nevertheless triumphantly bests the gunman in a fistfight before pausing, a true thespian, to declaim, 'These amateurs are the curse of my life.' Sophia Loren, blonde for a change, is enchanting as the flighty Angie, unable to stop flirting even though she knows she may lose Healy for good. There's excellent comedy from Heckart and O'Brien, constantly bickering, with Mrs Hathaway treating her daughter as a child in a vain attempt to preserve her own faded youth, and mortified when her daughter tells her to throw away all her little-girl clothes. 'I'm twenty years old,' protests Della. 'I'm dead already, my child just killed me . . . she's only sixteen,' moans her ageing mother.

There's a real feel for the absurdities of Victorian stage melodrama, and the costumes (by the great Edith Head) are splendid. In one astonishing scene, the Indians set upon the deserted wagons of the troupe and loot them, tossing gauzy strips of green and blue silk into the air, throwing pink and turquoise ostrich feathers up to the sky. Is *My Darling Clementine* (1946) the only other Western besides this one in which a character quotes lines from *Hamlet*?

Dir: George Cukor; **Prod**: Carlo Ponti, Marcello Girosi; **Scr**: Dudley Nichols, Walter Bernstein; **DOP**: Harold Lipstein; **Score**: Daniele Amfitheatrof.

Hell's Hinges
US, 1916 – 64 mins
Charles Swickard

Together with Tom Mix, William S. Hart was the most successful star of
the silent Western. Beginning in 1914, Hart appeared in over fifty films,
almost all of them Westerns. His standard role was as the good badman,
a stern-faced, strong and mostly silent hero, often initially on the wrong
side of the law. During the film he will undergo an epiphany, usually
through an encounter with a virginal young girl, and will then go on to
confront evil and root it out. This is the formula for *Hell's Hinges*, in
which Hart plays Blaze Tracey, a denizen of Hell's Hinges, 'a devil's den
of iniquity' out on the prairie. Blaze is rough and tough; his motto is
'Shoot first and do your disputin' afterwards.' A young parson (Jack
Standing), weak and ineffective, is sent to the town, accompanied by his
sister Faith (Clara Williams). Egged on by Silk Miller (Alfred
Hollingsworth), the local saloon-owner, who fears for his trade if the
parson gains influence, Blaze goes to scare the parson away but is
immediately smitten by the felicitously named Faith. When a bunch of
rowdies burst in on a church service, Blaze enters and clears them out at
gunpoint, as if in answer to the earnest prayers of the girl. 'When I look
at you, I feel I've been riding the wrong trail,' Blaze confesses. Blaze goes
home and starts reading the Bible, but Silk has another plan. He invites
the parson to come and preach to his dance-hall girls, and before long
one of them, Dolly (Louise Glaum), has got him smoking and drinking,
and eventually kissing her. Blaze and Faith retrieve the parson drunk from
the saloon and Blaze rides out of town for the doctor in order to help
him. But the next day, the parson returns to the saloon, where a drunken
mob proposes to burn down the church. Though the God-fearing
townspeople try to resist, the church is burned and the parson shot. At
this point, Blaze rides back into town. In the saloon he shoots Silk Miller
and holds the mob at bay while he sets fire to the building. Eventually, in
a deliberate act of righteous retribution, the whole town is set alight by

the now aptly named Blaze. After burying her brother, Faith and Blaze walk away together.

The religiosity of the film (such as a dissolve to a cross as Faith kneels in prayer) has dated it badly, but Hart still has charisma, his angular face embodying a stern morality that is in keeping with the code of the west. Unlike Mix, Hart was not brought up a cowboy, but instead learned his acting trade on the stage, playing in a theatrical version of Owen Wister's influential Western novel, *The Virginian*. But he does some hard riding on his horse Fritz and plenty of shooting in his trademark two-gun style. The finale, with the town ablaze, anticipates Clint Eastwood's *High Plains Drifter* (1972).

Dir: Charles Swickard; **Prod**: Thomas Ince; **Scr**: C. Gardner Sullivan; **DOP**: Joseph August.

High Noon
US, 1952 – 85 mins
Fred Zinnemann

Constructed with metronomic efficiency, this is a suspense film using the motivation of revenge which is so common in the Western. Will Kane (Gary Cooper) has just got married and is leaving his job as sheriff of Hadleyville, much to the relief of his Quaker wife Amy (Grace Kelly). But waiting at the station this Sunday morning is the gang of Frank Miller, whom Kane had put in jail some years ago. When the train arrives at noon with Miller aboard they intend to make Kane pay. Over the eighty-five minutes' duration (the film takes place in real time) Kane seeks to get some assistance, having informed Amy that he cannot avoid his responsibilities. As usual in the Western, the woman's role is to plead for peace, and Amy's response when Will refuses to avoid the coming confrontation is to announce she will leave him. Touring the town he encounters the judge who had condemned Miller; he is leaving town and advises Kane to do the same. Kane's deputy, Harvey Pell (Lloyd Bridges), makes it a condition of his support that Kane will ensure he will get the sheriff's job when he leaves, but Kane does not trust him. Kane also meets Helen Ramirez (Katy Jurado), Miller's former lover as well as Kane's, a dark-haired sultry counterpoint to the blonde and virginal Amy. A visit to the saloon gains him no useful assistance, and finally Kane enters the church to plead with the upright citizens. But they all find their own way of declining to join his cause. On the stroke of twelve the train arrives. Miller and his gang walk into town. In the ensuing gunfight, Kane manages to get the better of them, but only when his wife deserts her Quaker principles of non-violence and shoots one of them in the back. At the end, Kane drops his sheriff's badge in the street in disgust at the cowardice of the townsfolk, and he and Amy leave town.

Because screenwriter Carl Foreman was blacklisted after writing the film, *High Noon* has often been interpreted as an attack on McCarthyism: Kane is willing to stand up for what is right in the face of general indifference by the majority. However, it is equally possible to see the film as an endorsement of the necessity for strong individuals to fight the forces of evil, which might in 1952 have included international Communism. Director Fred Zinnemann always resisted a strict allegorical interpretation on the grounds that it unduly restricted the universal significance of his film.

If the constant shots of a ticking clock are over-emphatic, the film benefits greatly from a series of strong performances, especially from Gary Cooper, his deeply lined face (he was ailing at the time) expressive of determination in the face of disillusion, from the radiant Grace Kelly and the impressive Katy Jurado, as well as such ever-dependable bit players as Robert Wilke and Lee Van Cleef as Miller's henchmen. Cooper won the Oscar for Best Actor and Dimitri Tiomkin for Best Score, including the wonderfully evocative theme tune, sung by Tex Ritter.

Dir: Fred Zinnemann; **Prod**: Stanley Kramer; **Scr**: Carl Foreman; **DOP**: Floyd Crosby; **Score**: Dimitri Tiomkin.

High Plains Drifter
US, 1972 – 105 mins
Clint Eastwood

Not surprisingly, Eastwood's first Western as both star and director owes
something to his work with Sergio Leone. A mysterious stranger
(Eastwood) rides into the town of Lago and when an inhabitant asks,
'What did you say your name was again?' his reply is a curt 'I didn't.'
Like Leone's Man with No Name, he is quickly challenged by three
roughnecks, and despatches them in the blink of an eye. Unlike the
Leone character, he does have an interest in sex. When a young woman,
Callie (Marianna Hill), deliberately provokes him, he drags her into a
stable and rapes her. (Eastwood came to regret this scene, admitting it
was not politically correct and that later in his career he might not have
done it that way.)

Resting in his hotel room, he has a flashback to a man being set
upon at night. As the townspeople, intimidated by the stranger, discuss
what to do, their dirty secret emerges. The prosperity of the town
depends on a local mine; when the sheriff discovered the mine was on
federal property and threatened to disclose the fact, he was whipped to
death by three thugs hired for the purpose. These three men were then
turned over to the authorities; now they are being released from jail and
the townsfolk are terrified they will want revenge.

The plot has something in common with *High Noon* (1952), *Warlock*
(1959) and other films in which cowardly citizens turn against those who
try to impose law and order. But *High Plains Drifter* goes further. The
stranger demands dictatorial powers in exchange for his help, which he
uses to humiliate the townsfolk. As sheriff he instals a midget, Mordecai
(Billy Curtis, who had previously appeared as a munchkin in *The Wizard
of Oz* [1939], and also in the all-midget Western, *Terror of Tiny Town*
[1938]). He distributes blankets from the store to poor Indians, and treats
everyone to drinks at the saloon-owner's expense. Soon the citizens are
plotting how to get rid of him. Callie agrees to have sex with him again,

but sets him up to be attacked. Later he seduces Sarah (Verna Bloom), the wife of the hotel-owner; she and Mordecai appear to be the only ones willing to acknowledge what happened to the previous sheriff.

The stranger trains the townspeople to defend themselves, but as the three men approach to seek their revenge he leaves, having first ordered the town painted red and renamed it 'Hell'. After it has been ransacked by the three men, the stranger returns to the town and, having set light to it, picks them off one by one. The next morning he rides out, his mission accomplished.

Setting the town of 'Hell' alight is reminiscent of William S. Hart's silent classic *Hell's Hinges*, while the quasi-supernatural aspect of the story (is the stranger the sheriff's ghost?) would re-appear in Eastwood's *Pale Rider* (1985). It's an assured directorial debut for Eastwood, perfectly framed and paced, and with a stunning setting on the shores of Mono Lake in the California high desert.

Dir: Clint Eastwood; **Prod**: Robert Daley; **Scr**: Ernest Tidyman; **DOP**: Bruce Surtees; **Score**: Dee Barton.

The Iron Horse
US, 1924 – 134 mins
John Ford

After the success of Paramount's *The Covered Wagon* in 1923, Fox decided they too must have a Western epic, and clearly John Ford was the man to direct it. Ford begins his story in the 1840s in Springfield, Illinois, with local citizens discussing a transcontinental railroad in the presence of Abe Lincoln (Charles Edward Bull), who pronounces it an inevitable sign of progress. Two children, Davy and Miriam, are friends, but are parted when Davy's father takes him west. On the trail, Davy's father is murdered by Indians, led by a white man with missing fingers. The story moves to 1862; Lincoln is President and orders a railroad to connect the two coasts. One company, Central Pacific, starts from California, building through the Sierra Nevada; the other, Union Pacific, pushes westwards across the plains. Miriam (Madge Bellamy) is now engaged to Jesson (Cyril Chadwick), a surveyor with Union Pacific. Bauman (Fred Kohler), a big landowner, wants the railroad to run through his property and persuades Ruby (Gladys Hulette), a saloon girl, to seduce Jesson so that Bauman can exert influence over him. Davy discovers the plan and eventually confronts Bauman, who turns out to be the man with missing fingers who had murdered his father. Davy and Miriam are reunited just as the two halves of the railroad are joined together.

Ford had served his apprenticeship making Westerns with Harry Carey and Hoot Gibson, but this was his first attempt at the epic. It appears Ford never had a finished script for the film, merely an outline. But the large budget allowed him to shoot on location and put together some spectacular scenes, including the manhandling of a locomotive up a snowy Sierra mountain. Surprisingly for such an important production, Ford chose George O'Brien, an unknown athletics champion and stunt man, for the leading male role. Though he also starred in Murnau's *Sunrise* (1927), O'Brien's subsequent career was mostly in the B-Western,

with occasional small parts in later Ford films. By contrast, Madge
Bellamy was an established star of sophisticated comedies.

The Iron Horse has much in common with Ford's later Westerns,
including some broad comedy involving the Irish labourers working for
Union Pacific (led by Ford stalwart, J. Farrell MacDonald), a compelling
use of landscape, especially in Ford's characteristic long shots, and a
sense of history in the making while at the same time telling an intimate
personal story. The railroad is a means of restoring the unity of the
nation ruptured by the Civil War, and the means whereby Manifest

John Ford, director of The Iron Horse, reproduces Andrew Russell's famous photograph of
the joining of the rails from east and west in 1869

Destiny, the settlement of the entire continent, is to be achieved. This is celebrated in a reconstruction of the famous scene at Promontory Point in Utah, where the rails from east and west are finally joined together. Despite the large budget, Fox made a substantial profit when the film turned out a huge success, grossing $2 million, though Ford's attempt at another large-scale Western in 1926, *Three Bad Men*, did not fare so well.

Dir: John Ford; **Prod**: John Ford; **Scr**: Charles Kenyon; **DOP**: George Schneiderman.

Johnny Guitar
US, 1954 – 110mins
Nicholas Ray

The film was, from the start, intended as a vehicle for its star, Joan Crawford, who exerted great influence throughout the production. According to the scriptwriter, Philip Yordan, halfway through shooting, and apparently jealous of the attention being paid to her co-star Mercedes McCambridge, Crawford insisted that her role as Vienna be made into something more like a traditional male lead. Director Nicholas Ray had little choice but to agree, and Republic Pictures, the film's penurious producer, couldn't afford to have Crawford walk out. It is this shift in emphasis which makes *Johnny Guitar* such an unusual picture.

Johnny Guitar (Sterling Hayden) arrives at a gambling saloon owned by Vienna (originally the script explained her name by reference to her middle-European musical father; this was cut, but the alert viewer will notice a bust of Beethoven in her room). Vienna and Johnny were once lovers. Now the railroad is coming through town and Vienna stands to make a lot of money. But the local big rancher, McIvers (Ward Bond), doesn't want any railroad bringing in dirt farmers. Together with the sheriff and Emma (Mercedes McCambridge), he bursts into Vienna's saloon looking for a gang who have robbed the stage. Emma is half-crazed with jealousy of Vienna's current lover, the Dancing Kid (Scott Brady), and accuses him of the robbery. Vienna pulls a gun and eventually the posse leave, but not before McIvers has given Vienna and the Dancing Kid twenty-four hours to leave town. Thinking they have little to lose, the Kid and his gang rob the local bank. The gang takes refuge in a mine, its entrance hidden behind a waterfall, but the youngest member, Turkey (Ben Cooper) is captured by the posse. Having burned down Vienna's saloon, the posse hang Turkey and are

(*Opposite page*) Black-clad Joan Crawford as Vienna with Sterling Hayden as the eponymous Johnny Guitar

about to hang Vienna when she is rescued by Johnny Guitar. In a final shootout the Dancing Kid is shot by Emma, who is then killed by Vienna.

A melodrama with all the stops pulled out, the film has a bold colour scheme, contrasting the red deserts of Sedona, Arizona, where it was mostly shot, the funeral black of the posse, and Vienna seated at the piano in a white dress, the only colour the red gash of her mouth. It also benefits from a wonderful theme song, sung over the conclusion by Peggy Lee. But *Johnny Guitar* has achieved cult status largely because of its subversion of gender roles. In the concluding shootout, Vienna, gunbelt strapped round her waist, confronts the black-clad Emma, also wearing a gun. That these two are the toughest characters in the picture cannot be doubted. 'Never seen a woman who was more like a man,' one character remarks of Vienna, redundantly. Vienna herself is all too aware of sexual stereotyping: 'All a woman has to do is slip once and she's a tramp.' Johnny Guitar, by contrast, is a curiously passive creation, coolly delivering his laidback philosophy: 'When you boil it all down, what does a man really need? Just a smoke and a cup of coffee.'

Dir: Nicholas Ray; **Prod**: Herbert J. Yates; **Scr**: Philip Yordan; **DOP**: Harry Stradling; **Score**: Victor Young.

The Last of the Mohicans
US, 1992 – 122 mins
Michael Mann

Based, albeit loosely, upon James Fenimore Cooper's classic novel, often claimed as the founding work of the fictional west, *The Last of the Mohicans* also acknowledges an earlier film version from 1936, which starred Randolph Scott as Cooper's hero Natty Bumppo, or Hawkeye. In this later version, Daniel Day-Lewis plays the frontiersman, brought up among Indians, with one foot in civilisation and one in the wilderness. It is 1757. Cora (Madeleine Stowe) and Alice (Jodhi May) are the daughters of Colonel Munro (Maurice Roëves), who is besieged by the French and their Indian allies at Fort William Henry. Hawkeye and his Indian companions, Uncas (Eric Schweig) and his father Chingachgook (Russell Means) rescue the girls from the clutches of the treacherous Indian Magua (Wes Studi) and deliver them to the fort, where Hawkeye and Cora form an attachment. Outgunned, Munro is forced to surrender. Though assured of safe passage by the French, the British column is set upon by the Indians after leaving the fort. Munro is killed by Magua, who has a grudge against him, and his two daughters are captured. Hawkeye and his friends set off in pursuit. Uncas, who has fallen in love with Alice, is killed by Magua trying to rescue her. Seeing this, Alice jumps to her death, but Chingachgook in turn kills Magua.

The principal plot alteration from Cooper's work is that originally it is Cora who becomes attached to Uncas. Though an officer's daughter, she has a darker skin because her mother was West Indian, thus in Cooper's eyes neutralising the difficult issue of racial mixing. In the novel, Hawkeye has no romantic entanglement; Hollywood demands that its heroes fall in love, but in having Uncas involved not with Cora, merely with Alice, a minor character, Michael Mann can also be accused of ducking out of the issue of miscegenation.

The film makes a point of playing up the stresses between the British and the American colonists. Major Duncan Heyward (Steven

Waddington), Cora's disappointed suitor, is a snob and unsympathetic to the sturdy independence of the colonists, who, as Hawkeye explains, are on the frontier because 'they're beholden to none'. The British sneer at the French ('They'd rather eat and make love with their faces than fight,' says one officer), but British soldiers prove no match for the Indians in open combat. Instead it is the frontiersman and his Indian companions who save the day.

Like *Dances With Wolves* a couple of years before, *The Last of the Mohicans* casts Native Americans in the principal Indian roles, and at times uses subtitles to translate native languages. But the film is essentially an old-fashioned adventure story, filmed with great verve and gusto. The action sequences are brilliantly staged, the use of landscape (the film was mostly shot in the Carolinas) stunning and the acting generally excellent, with Wes Studi outstanding as a truly malevolent Magua. The music, originally by Trevor Jones, with Randy Edelman being brought in after creative differences with the director, manages the difficult feat of being highly romantic yet with a period feel.

Dir: Michael Mann; **Prod**: Michael Mann, Hunt Lowry; **Scr**: Michael Mann, Christopher Crowe; **DOP**: Dante Spinotti; **Score**: Trevor Jones, Randy Edelman.

The Last Sunset
US, 1961 – 112 mins
Robert Aldrich

Sheriff Dana Stribling (Rock Hudson) comes down to Mexico in pursuit of a wanted man. As the film progresses, we discover that this man has killed his brother-in-law, as a result of which Stribling's sister committed suicide. His quarry is Brendan O'Malley (Kirk Douglas), a charming but dangerous black-clad gunfighter who carries a derringer in his belt. O'Malley turns up at the ranch of Belle Breckenridge (Dorothy Malone), O'Malley's former sweetheart now married to a drunken ex-Confederate soldier (Joseph Cotten). Belle rebuffs him, but her daughter, Missie (Carol Lynley), is seduced by O'Malley's eloquence and sophistication. Breckenridge wants to drive his cattle north to Texas and O'Malley agrees to help him in return for one fifth of the proceeds, believing he can persuade Belle to take him back. When Stribling arrives to take O'Malley prisoner, he is persuaded to join the cattle drive too, as the best way of getting the wanted man into Texas, where he can be arrested. Stribling contemptuously denounces O'Malley to Belle ('He can't tell one female from another, and he don't much care either'). Breckenridge is shot dead in a Mexican cantina by some former fellow-soldiers who accuse him of cowardice, but the cattle drive continues. Belle tells O'Malley that he still wants her to be the young innocent girl he remembers rather than the mature woman she has become; by now Stribling has fallen for Belle and wants to marry her. After adventures along the trail with Indians and some shifty characters who want to kidnap the two women, the herd reaches the Rio Grande. That night Missie tries to persuade O'Malley to make love to her and after initially telling her she is too young he kisses her passionately. But once they are in Texas, Belle tells O'Malley that Missie is really his daughter. O'Malley and Stribling face each other in a gunfight, but after O'Malley is shot Stribling discovers that his derringer contained no bullet.

What could have been a ludicrously melodramatic tale is given real intensity by the direction and performances. In a role tailor-made for him,

Douglas excels as the charmer with a mean streak just below the surface, whose compulsion to seduce women provokes his daughter's incestuous infatuation and thus leads to his suicide, a fitting payback for the death of Stribling's sister. Malone is also excellent as a woman desperately trying to break free of the past, only to watch in horror as her daughter seems compelled to repeat it, even to the extent of dressing up for O'Malley in the yellow dress Belle wore when she last saw him. Aldrich nicely balances the rhythms of the cattle drive with moments of drama, such as Stribling's horse sinking in a quicksand while O'Malley bargains with him. The title, evocative as it is of the end of the west, seems to have no particular relevance to the film.

Dir: Robert Aldrich; **Prod**: Eugene Frenke, Edward Lewis; **Scr**: Dalton Trumbo; **DOP**: Ernest Laszlo; **Score**: Ernest Gold.

The Last Wagon
US, 1956 – 99 mins
Delmer Daves

Richard Widmark started his screen career as a sneering villain and in the role of Comanche Todd, *The Last Wagon* makes good use of the mean streak in his screen persona. We first encounter him on foot, being hunted down in the Arizona wilderness. He's been three days without food or water, say his pursuers. Though he manages to knife one of them he is finally captured by a sadistic sheriff, who drags him behind his horse. The sheriff intends to take him back to be hanged for murder, and enjoys telling him of a previous hanging where the victim took half an hour to die. But when they run into a wagon train of Christian emigrants, the sheriff is forced to mitigate his cruelty to Todd. Jenny (Felicia Farr) insists he is a human being, but the sheriff tells her that though Todd may be white, inside he is all Comanche, an 'injun-loving murderer'.

The leader of the wagon train has two daughters; one, Jolie (Susan Kohner), is by his second wife, a Navajo, and is hated by the other daughter Valinda (Stephanie Griffin). Valinda is an out-and-out racist who talks of 'filthy Indians' and is hostile to Todd. Despite being chained to a wagon wheel, Todd manages to kill the sheriff, his tormentor, with an axe. Later that night, the two daughters go swimming with some boys. When they return they find that Apaches have attacked the wagons and killed everyone except Todd, who agrees to try and lead them to safety, though the Indians are all around. Along the trail it emerges that Todd's Indian wife and two sons were murdered by whites. Todd defeats two Apaches in hand-to-hand fighting and gradually the racists in the party come to feel gratitude for his help. One night Todd makes love to Jenny ('I didn't know Comanches kissed like this,' she says). Though they meet up with some soldiers, they are still only a handful against 300 Apaches, but Todd devises a plan to blow up the wagons and they escape. Back in civilisation Todd is brought before the

Bible-reading General Howard (a character who appears in Daves' *Broken Arrow* [1950]), who engages him in a debate about the ethics of revenge. Todd explains that he killed the men who raped and murdered his wife and killed his sons; after Jenny and the others plead for him, he is allowed to go free.

Splendidly shot in spectacular locations, *The Last Wagon* is sustained by Widmark's performance, mixing charm and menace. Farr looks fetching in brown leather trousers, and though the romance is conventional, there is more than a hint of miscegenation (the blonde Todd is not actually an Indian, but is strongly identified with Indians). Indeed, the exploration of racism is more compelling than in *Broken Arrow*. Todd is less obviously 'noble' than Cochise, and a more interesting character, while the antagonism of characters like Valinda towards Indians is shockingly visceral.

Dir: Delmer Daves; **Prod**: William B. Hawks; **Scr**: James Edward Grant, Delmer Daves, Gwen Bagni Gielgud; **DOP**: Wilfred M. Cline; **Score**: Lionel Newman.

The Law and Jake Wade
US, 1958 – 86 mins
John Sturges

Sometimes the films of John Sturges, never less than efficiently directed, can be lacking in genuine emotional involvement. But *The Law and Jake Wade* builds genuine drama out of the conflict between its two antagonists. Jake Wade (Robert Taylor) rides into a small town and busts Clint Hollister (Richard Widmark) out of jail. Once out of town Wade says they are now quits and goes his own way. We discover that he is in fact a sheriff in another town. Engaged to marry Peggy (Patricia Owens), he tries to persuade her they should move further west, but will not explain why. Then Clint reappears, together with his gang, including the unstable Rennie (Henry Silva), black-leather-clad Wexler (DeForest Kelley) and Ortero (Robert Middleton). They take Jake and Peggy prisoner and ride off. On the

Clint (Richard Widmark) and Jake (Robert Taylor) reach a showdown in *The Law and Jake Wade*, with Ortero (Robert Middleton) caught in the middle

trail it emerges that Jake and Clint had been irregulars in a Confederate guerrilla band during the Civil War, and had continued to rob banks after the war's end. But Jake had ridden away when he believed he had killed a child in a raid, burying the proceeds and eventually going straight.

Now, under the threat of violence towards Peggy, Clint intends to force Jake to tell him where the money is hidden. Clint sadistically keeps Jake's hands tightly bound as they ride. Peggy realises the danger she and Jake are in when Rennie tells her that the first man he killed was his own father. Meeting with a group of cavalry, they are warned of the danger of Indians, but proceed on to the ghost town where Jake has buried the money. Then the Indians appear. Jake starts working on the nerves of the gang, overturning their belief that Indians will not attack at night. That's only true of Apaches, he says; 'These are Comanches.' Both Rennie and Wexler are killed by the Indians, but though Jake gets free Clint gets the drop on him and forces him to dig up the money. What Clint doesn't expect is that there is a gun hidden in the bag. Jake says it is time he and Clint settled their differences and throws Clint a gun. 'I would have handed one to you,' Clint protests. 'Well, you like me a lot better than I like you,' says Jake. All along Clint has been boasting of his superior shooting skills, but he finds too late that he has over-estimated himself.

Widmark excels as the smiling villain with the mean streak, sneering equally at the 'scenic grandeur' of the mountains and at Jake's manifest decency. 'I suppose you're talking about something like honour, which is supposed to be too deep for me to understand.' It's clear that Clint knows Jake is the better man, which makes him even meaner. Taylor is excellent too as the wary Jake, watching for an opening, troubled by Peggy's discovery of his past but determined to protect her from the likes of Rennie, whose salacious remarks make his intentions clear. Shot in CinemaScope, the film revels in the harsh but beautiful desert landscape.

Dir: John Sturges; **Prod**: William Hawks; **Scr**: William Bowers; **DOP**: Robert Surtees; **Score**: no credit given.

Little Big Man
US, 1970 – 147 mins
Arthur Penn

In a retirement home a wizened old man, allegedly aged 121, recounts his life story to an earnest young researcher. Jack Crabbe (Dustin Hoffman) recalls how he was first captured by Cheyenne Indians as a child. Jack finds Indian life fun and is adopted into the tribe by Old Lodge Skins (Chief Dan George), but after a few years is forcibly removed back to the white side of the racial divide. His subsequent career is a pattern of crossings from one culture to the other, but Jack has no doubt which side he prefers. In a series of picaresque adventures, he encounters a hypocritical preacher, the Rev. Pendrake (Thayer David) and his lascivious wife (Faye Dunaway), who undertakes Jack's sexual initiation, as well as Merriweather (Martin Balsam), a shifty seller of quack remedies and Wild Bill Hickok (Jeff Corey), who teaches him how to be a gunfighter. Jack marries, but is once again captured by Indians, whose society he perceives as far superior. Whereas white society is generally venal and corrupt, by contrast, the Cheyenne are strong on spirituality, affectionate and pleasure-loving, and tolerant of sexual nonconformity. Old Lodge Skins is a wise and loving father figure, and soon Jack acquires an Indian wife, Sunshine (Amy Eccles), to replace the white one. But the Cheyenne camp is attacked by the army under General Custer (Richard Mulligan) and Sunshine is killed. Returning once more to white society, Jack observes the shooting of Wild Bill in Deadwood in 1876. Enrolling as a muleskinner in Custer's service, Jack encourages him to take on the Indians at the Little Big Horn river, with satisfying consequences. After the battle, Jack finds Old Lodge Skins once more.

Based on Thomas Berger's wonderfully wry and inventive novel, *Little Big Man* gives a highly innovative twist to the traditional captivity narrative such as that which sustains *The Searchers* (1956), with the repeated comings and goings of Jack across the line providing multiple opportunities for cultural comparisons. These are very much of their time.

The Cheyenne are New Age Indians, a complete antidote to the materialism, aggression and sexual inhibitions of contemporary America. Custer, by contrast, is a half-crazed racist imperialist whose arrogance leads him to his doom. The Seventh Cavalry's attack on the Cheyenne at the Washita (based on an historical incident) has clear reference to the events of the Vietnam War (the Mylai massacre became public knowledge in 1969). Sustained by a literate and witty script, and a series

The lascivious Mrs Pendrake (Faye Dunaway) gives the young Jack Crabb (Dustin Hoffman) a bath in *Little Big Man*

of striking performances, not least by Dustin Hoffman in a role that requires him to age about 100 years, this is a highly enjoyable film, as well as a politically correct antidote to Hollywood's previous dealings with the Indian 'problem'. It made a star out of Chief Dan George, one of the first genuine Native American actors to have a substantial role in a major Hollywood film.

Dir: Arthur Penn; **Prod**: Stuart Millar; **Scr**: Calder Willingham; **DOP**: Harry Stradling Jr; **Score**: John Hammond.

Lonesome Cowboys
US, 1968 – 110 mins
Andy Warhol

After its showing at the San Francisco Film Festival in 1968, FBI agents
opened a file on *Lonesome Cowboys* which read, in part:

> All the males in the cast displayed homosexual tendencies and conducted
> themselves toward one another in an effeminate manner. One of the cowboys
> practised his ballet and a conversation ensued regarding the misuse of
> mascara by one of the other cowboys. There was no plot to the film and no
> development of character throughout. It was rather a remotely connected
> series of scenes which depicted situations of sexual relationships of a
> homosexual and heterosexual nature.

This is an accurate description as far as it goes, though it fails to capture
the unique flavour of the Andy Warhol film experience. The film opens
with Ramona (Warhol 'superstar' Viva) having sex with Julian (Tom
Hompertz), accompanied on the soundtrack by a pastiche Western ballad
('Lonesome Cowboy, You Won't Be Lonesome with Me'). Then a group
of cowboys enter a rundown Western town. Ramona, who is the town
prostitute, appears in a black riding outfit, together with her 'nurse'
(Taylor Meade) and they make personal remarks about the cowboys'
appearance ('He's cute'), while the cowboys themselves hold a series of
desultory conversations about haircuts and the correct posture for
wearing a gun ('It puts meat on your buns').

    As Mark Finch has said, the film can't really be bothered to be either
a porn film or a concerted attempt at exploring the homosexual subtext
of the Western, though it gestures languorously towards both aims. The
cowboys talk endlessly, besides bickering and engaging in horseplay. But
they don't actually get it on with each other. The camera likes to look at
them, and there's one protracted scene of Julian stripping down and
taking a wash, but the only sex we see is between Viva and one or other

of the cowboys; at one point several of them strip her and threaten to rape her, but they're all fags, she says dismissively. The sheriff (Francis Francine) is a cross-dresser and spends a lot of time putting on his make-up and corset, but the suggestions of a proper Western plot at the start (cowboys riding into town and disrupting the local citizens, who demand the sheriff takes action) are not followed through.

Hardcore gay pornography has consistently mined the Western genre, rendering explicit the homosexual subtext that runs through it, making the most of the erotic potential of denim and leather, and the obvious phallic implications of guns. But none of this is much referenced in *Lonesome Cowboys*. Instead, there's a curious blankness in many of the scenes between Joe Dallesandro, Tom Hompertz and the other pretty boys, which seems to be the point. By contrast, Viva is often entertainingly risqué, especially in her monologue about Catholic rituals, delivered while persuading Hompertz to disrobe ('Would God have left his pants on?'), and Taylor Meade, who appears to be stoned throughout the entire film, supplies some amusing if conventionally campy moments.

Dir: Andy Warhol; **Prod**: Andy Warhol; **Scr**: Andy Warhol; **DOP**: Paul Morrissey.

The Long Riders
US, 1980 – 100 mins
Walter Hill

There are a score or more Jesse James Westerns; among the most
memorable are *Jesse James* (1939), with Tyrone Power in the title role,
The True Story of Jesse James (1957), with Robert Wagner as Jesse, and
The Great Northfield Minnesota Road (1972), with Robert Duvall as the
legendary outlaw. But on balance, *The Long Riders* is the best. The
casting appears at first sight to be a gimmick. Four sets of brothers play
the principal roles, with David, Keith and Robert Carradine playing Cole,
Jim and Bob Younger, James and Stacy Keach as Jesse and Frank James,
Dennis and Randy Quaid as Ed and Clel Miller, and Christopher and
Nicholas Guest as Charlie and Bob Ford. In practice, the casting is greatly
to the film's advantage, since it reinforces its conception of the outlaw
gang as a close-knit group held tightly together by family ties. A
Pinkerton man acknowledges that this makes it difficult to catch them.
Yet, at the same time, it is this very closeness that is ultimately Jesse's
undoing. At the beginning of the film, Jesse expels Ed Miller from the
gang because he has panicked during a bank robbery. Ed's brother Clel
remains loyal to Jesse. When at Jesse's wedding to Zee (Savannah Smith
Boucher), Frank and Cole are approached by the Ford brothers, trying to
ingratiate themselves, it is made painfully clear to them that they are
outsiders. At the funeral of Jesse's young brother (murdered by the
Pinkertons), the Fords again try to break into the gang, only to be once
more spurned. Their exclusion engenders resentment.

Unlike most other versions, this film ignores the legend that Jesse
gave his money away to the poor; the Pinkertons claim that such stories
are myths made up by the newspapers. (A reporter pops up from time to
time, assiduously gathering facts and asking awkward questions.) But
The Long Riders follows tradition in making much of Jesse's allegiance to
the southern cause in the Civil War. At gunpoint Clel forces a musician
to replace 'The Battle Cry of Freedom' with 'I'm a Good Old Rebel'. At

the end, in prison, Bob Younger tells the Pinkertons, 'We done it for Dixie and nothing else.'

The two central characters, Jesse and Cole, are contrasted in their attitudes to sexuality. Jesse marries his childhood sweetheart after a lengthy courtship. Cole prefers whores, in particular the feisty Belle Starr (Pamela Reed). On the last night before the fateful Northfield raid, the gang stay at a brothel. When Jesse abstains, Cole sneers at his loyalty to Zee. Jesse is fiercely resentful.

Eventually Jesse pays for his treatment of the Fords, who accept blood money to shoot him in the back as he sets straight a sampler embroidered with the words 'God bless our home'. It's a perfunctory ending to a film of great verve and style, especially in the action set-pieces such as a train robbery and the Northfield raid itself. Throughout, the film is greatly enriched by Ry Cooder's wonderful score, evoking a real feel of time and place by drawing on traditional motifs.

Dir: Walter Hill; **Prod**: Tim Zinnemann; **Scr**: Bill Bryden, Steven P. Smith, Stacy and James Keach; **DOP**: Ric Waite; **Score**: Ry Cooder.

The Magnificent Seven
US, 1960 – 138 mins
John Sturges

A highly successful film on the international market, this may be seen as a precursor of the Italian Westerns of the 1960s. Based, like Leone's *A Fistful of Dollars* (1964), on a film by the Japanese director Akira Kurosawa (in this case *The Seven Samurai* [1954]), its heroes are, like Leone's Man with No Name, mercenaries offering their guns to the highest bidder. A Mexican village is under constant threat from the bandit Calvera (Eli Wallach) and peasants come north to buy protection. First to enlist is Chris (Yul Brynner). The character of each subsequent

The Magnificent Seven (left to right): Chris (Yul Brynner), Vin (Steve McQueen), Chico (Horst Buchholz), Bernardo (Charles Bronson), Lee (Robert Vaughn), Harry (Brad Dexter), Britt (James Coburn)

recruit is deftly sketched in as Chris enrols them: the coldly clinical knife-fighter Britt (James Coburn), the affable Vin (Steve McQueen), the black-clad gunfighter Lee (Robert Vaughan), whose nerves have been shattered by the stress of his occupation, O'Reilly (Charles Bronson), half-Mexican, half-Irish, Harry (Brad Dexter), a gambler with a nose for money and Chico (Horst Buchholz), a naive young Mexican.

Down in Mexico, the seven organise the villagers to resist, but after initial success they are betrayed to Calvera. Surprisingly he lets them go, fearing reprisals from their friends, but the seven have had their pride stung and they return to take on the bandits. Heavily outnumbered, they eventually prevail but only three are left alive to return north of the border.

Sturges' direction of the action scenes is thrillingly stylish, making excellent use of the wide screen, and the script is loaded with the laconic philosophy of the world-weary seven, as when Vin, asked by Calvera why he has taken the job, recounts the story of the man in El Paso. 'One day, he just took all his clothes off and jumped in a mess of cactus. I asked him that same question, "Why?"' 'And?' 'He said, "It seemed like a good idea at the time."' Eli Wallach relishes the part of Calvera, played as the apotheosis of the cynical, deviously grinning Mexican bandit, a fitting opponent for the seven. Elmer Bernstein's stirring music has become one of the best known of all Western film scores. Perhaps the only weakness of the film is the somewhat mawkish romance between Chico and Petra (Rosenda Monteros), a waif-like peasant girl from the village.

With the benefit of hindsight it is tempting to see the film as an allegory of the Vietnam conflict. Acting upon a request from a Third World country, a group of American professionals agree to help defeat aggression, setting out to win hearts and minds and to train the locals to defend themselves. But, let down by the lack of a will to fight, the Americans are ultimately forced to withdraw (although in the film victory is theirs). However, if this is the intended meaning of the film, it is astonishingly prescient, since in 1960 American military forces were as yet only marginally involved in Vietnam. Better, perhaps, to see it as the forerunner of the European Western in which self-sufficient heroes perform balletic acts of violence amid vistas of Mexican deserts.

Dir: John Sturges; **Prod**: John Sturges; **Scr**: William Roberts; **DOP**: Charles B. Lang Jr; **Score**: Elmer Bernstein.

Major Dundee
US, 1964 – 136 mins
Sam Peckinpah

As so often, Peckinpah fell out with his producers, and as a result *Major Dundee* was edited against his wishes. In *Horizons West*, Jim Kitses details the scenes that were omitted, but a recent re-issue on DVD has restored some of the missing material, thus further enhancing what is a major work by the greatest director of Westerns since John Ford.

Major Dundee (Charlton Heston) has been put in charge of a Union prison camp during the Civil War, a demotion for some unspecified act of recklessness at Gettysburg. When an Apache raid carries off some white children, the Major wishes to give pursuit, but hasn't enough men. He decides to recruit from among the criminals in his jail, and also from the Confederate prisoners it holds. Among these is Captain Tyreen (Richard Harris), who has been cashiered from the army before the war, largely at Dundee's instigation. Despite the mutual hatred between the two men, Tyreen volunteers for the mission after Dundee threatens to hang him for the murder of a guard. Dundee's command is divided from the start, signalled in the different songs the troops sing as they ride out: 'Dixie' for the southerners, 'John Brown's Body' for the Union troops and 'Clementine' for the civilians.

Dundee and Tyreen continue their bitter feud as they ride into Mexico in search of the Apaches. Dundee considers Tyreen a hopeless romantic, 'a would-be cavalier, an Irish potato farmer with a plumed hat fighting for a white-columned plantation house you've never had and never will'. Tyreen believes Dundee to be an ambitious man sacrificing others for his own advancement. Ambushed by the Apaches, the survivors have to rest up in a Mexican village, which they liberate from the occupying French troops of Maximilian. Here they discover a beautiful Austrian widow, Teresa (Senta Berger), whom both Tyreen and Dundee court. After recklessly swimming with her outside the picket lines (and, one assumes, having sex), Dundee is shot in the thigh

Dallying with Teresa (Senta Berger) outside his picket lines, Major Dundee (Charlton Heston) gets an Apache arrow in the thigh

by an Apache arrow. He is taken in secret to a doctor in Durango and while recovering, descends into drunken self-disgust, made worse when Teresa discovers him with a Mexican whore. Rejoining his command, Dundee devises a ruse to entice the Apaches into a fight, but afterwards, when the Americans reach the river that forms the border, their way back is blocked by French lancers. Dundee leads a charge against them, but only a few of his men make it across to the USA.

With an eloquent script and outstanding acting, not only from the principals but also many Peckinpah regulars such as the excellent James Coburn as the scout, Sam Potts, *Major Dundee* powerfully blends its character-driven narrative with a perceptive commentary on the Civil War. The issues of the war are ever present, and the film does not shrink from the racism of the southerners towards the black members of the troop. But Tyreen, having damned the Union flag, seizes it at the last and gallops in a brave but futile gesture into the heart of the French forces.

Dir: Sam Peckinpah; **Prod**: Jerry Bresler; **Scr**: Harry Julian Fink, Oscar Saul, Sam Peckinpah; **DOP**: Sam Leavitt; **Score**: Daniele Amfitheatrof.

The Man from Laramie
US, 1955 – 101 mins
Anthony Mann

The last of the five Westerns which Anthony Mann made with James Stewart, arguably the best, and certainly the most visually stylish. Will Lockhart (Stewart) has come to New Mexico in search of those responsible for the death of his brother, a soldier killed by Indians armed with new repeating rifles. Having made a friend of Barbara Waggoman (Cathy O'Donnell), he then falls foul of her spiteful and neurotic cousin Dave (Alex Nicol). Dave's father is Alec (Donald Crisp), a patriarchal rancher who tries to deal with his wayward son through his trusted foreman Vic (Arthur Kennedy). Vic is beginning to turn against Alec because he feels that his service is not being adequately rewarded. Lockhart eventually uncovers a conspiracy between Vic and Dave to sell guns to the Indians. After Vic is forced to kill Dave, Lockhart and Vic have a final confrontation on a mountain-top.

As usual in Mann's Westerns, the psychological conflicts are essentially family ones, with oedipal overtones. It's no accident that Mann was contemplating a Western version of *King Lear*, Alec's manipulation of his sons, both natural and surrogate, being of a kind with Lear's toying with his daughters' affections. The film pushes to the limit Mann's preoccupation with the almost pathological desire of his heroes for vengeance and with the quasi-masochistic suffering they are forced to endure in their search for it. In a series of three powerful scenes, Mann dramatises in visceral fashion the extreme mental states which give his Westerns such emotional power. At their first meeting, marvellously staged on some glaring white salt flats, with Lockhart loading his wagon while Dave and his cronies ride closer along the skyline, Lockhart is humiliated by being roped and dragged behind a horse as his wagon is set on fire. Later in town there is a fistfight between the two, Lockhart giving Dave a savage beating as they struggle beneath the hooves of milling horses. And then, when he tries to ambush Lockhart, Dave gets shot in the hand. Ordering his ranch-hands to hold Lockhart prisoner, he deliberately extracts a vicious revenge by putting a bullet into Lockhart's outstretched hand. 'You – scum!' Lockhart hisses, his agony matched only by his contempt.

This is Mann's first Western in CinemaScope and he shows himself a master of the format, framing Lockhart at the centre of wide open spaces, emphasising his vulnerability both on the salt flats and later when

Will Lockhart (James Stewart) surveys the ruins of his burned-out wagons in *The Man from Laramie*

Dave shoots him in the hand. His use of landscape is exemplary; if Ford is the poet of the desert, Mann is the maestro of the mountains. Dave and Vic have hidden a consignment of rifles at the top of a lofty peak, and as the plot reaches its conclusion the camera continually follows upwards as horses and men strain to reach their goal, the physical and the psychological each perfectly expressed in the staging.

Dir: Anthony Mann; **Prod**: William Goetz; **Scr**: Philip Yordan, Frank Burt; **DOP**: Charles B. Lang Jr; **Score**: George Duning.

Man of the West
US, 1958 – 100 mins
Anthony Mann

Anthony Mann's cycle of Westerns with James Stewart is justly celebrated, but perhaps *Man of the West* is even better. An ageing Gary Cooper plays Link Jones, who is first presented as an amiable hick travelling by train to interview a teacher for his local school. On the train he meets Billie (Julie London), a dance-hall girl, and Beasley (Arthur O'Connell), a loquacious gambler. What began as an idyllic train ride through pretty scenery suddenly turns into a nightmare when, after the train is held up, Link, Billie and Beasley are accidentally left behind, apparently in the middle of nowhere.

Leading them to a lonely ranch house, Link gradually reveals that his past life was very different. He had been a member of a vicious gang of outlaws, commanded by the fearsome Dock Tobin (Lee J. Cobb), who had been a father-figure to him: 'He taught me killing and stealing.' It is into their clutches that Link now delivers himself and his companions, forced to pretend that he has returned on purpose. One of the gang, Coaley (Jack Lord), Link's cousin, forces Billie to strip and intends to rape her, but is prevented by Dock, who confides to Link his contempt for the gang. He dearly wants to believe that Link has come back to him. Later Coaley and Link fight and Link humiliates Coaley by stripping his clothes off him. In a frenzy, Link almost kills Coaley but cannot quite bring himself to.

Dock lives almost entirely in the past ('Do you remember Uvalde?'), and his scheme to rob a bank in the town of Lasso is based on his memory of how it used to be. In fact it is a ghost town ('That's what you are, a ghost,' Link tells him, 'you've outlived your time'). Once the gang assembles there, Link systematically destroys them: the mute Trout (Royal Dano), the brutish Ponch (Robert Wilke) and Claude (John Dehner), more intelligent than the rest and thus more dangerous. This sets up the final confrontation with Dock, who rapes Billie as a deliberate act of violence against Link. (Link has explained to Billie that he has a wife and family; she is drawn to him, but recognises that she cannot keep what she has found.) As so often with Mann, the climactic fight pits the good man against an opponent in a physically superior position, with Dock high up in the rocks, thus setting him up for a literal downfall.

Lee J. Cobb's bombastic acting style works well in the role of Dock, a larger than life figure who, though frighteningly evil, maintains some dignity and self-respect, something his band of grotesques conspicuously lacks. Cooper is simply wonderful as his face registers the anguish of seeing his past life thrust before his face, or is forced to watch Billie being stripped while a knife is held to his throat. Handsomely shot in CinemaScope, the film moves from initially verdant landscapes to the harsh desert of the final scenes.

Dir: Anthony Mann; **Prod**: Walter M. Mirisch; **Scr**: Reginald Rose; **DOP**: Ernest Haller; **Score**: Leigh Harline.

The Man Who Shot Liberty Valance
US, 1962 – 122 mins
John Ford

Ford's penultimate Western has a strongly elegiac feel. Like several others of this period, it's both about the end of the west and about the illusory myths which sustained it. Opening with a distant train chugging through the landscape, it tells its story in a lengthy flashback to a previous era when the west was wild. Ransom Stoddard (James Stewart), a naive young student of law, arrives in the town of Shinbone and is immediately beaten and robbed by Liberty Valance (Lee Marvin), the black-leather-clad outlaw who terrorises the locality. Stoddard meets Tom Doniphon (John Wayne), a local rancher and the only person tough enough to stand up to Valance. Doniphon is courting Hallie (Vera Miles); Stoddard gets a job in her parents' restaurant and teaches her to read, thereby supplanting Doniphon in her affections.

While gifted with all Ford's marvellously concrete characterisation and staging, the film is structured on a series of abstract oppositions: between violence and the law; between the desert wilderness of the untamed frontier and the garden it will become, symbolised in the cactus rose Doniphon gives to Hallie; between education and book-learning, as represented by Stoddard, and instinct as represented both by Doniphon and by Valance.

Eventually, despite his civilising mission, which extends to explaining the principles of Jeffersonian democracy to the local citizenry, including Doniphon's black servant Pompey (Woody Strode), Stoddard cannot avoid a confrontation with Valance. Hopelessly ill equipped for a gunfight, he steps out onto the street and to his and everyone's surprise emerges victorious. It is here that another structuring opposition is brought into play, that of myth and reality. Unknown to Stoddard, Doniphon has hidden himself just off the street, and at the climactic moment shoots Valance dead just as he is about to kill Stoddard. The latter goes on to trade on his celebrity, eventually becoming the state's

senator, while Doniphon declines into obscurity. The story of this deception is recounted to the local newspaper editor, who delivers one of the most celebrated, if gnomic utterances in the genre: 'This is the west, sir. When the legend becomes fact, print the legend.' This appears to mean that we need the inspiration of myth, and should not let the hard facts get in the way of our belief in heroes. Yet in demonstrating to the audience just how a myth has been constructed, Ford himself demystifies the west.

Shot in black and white (apparently for budgetary reasons as much as aesthetic), and for once avoiding the desert landscapes that are so much Ford's signature, the film has a dated, almost archaic look. But the mood is enlivened by a series of memorable performances, in the minor roles as much as in the leading parts: John Qualen as Hallie's Scandinavian immigrant father, Lee Van Cleef and Strother Martin as Valance's weasel-like sidekicks, Andy Devine as the cowardly, portly Marshal Link Appleyard, and above all Edmund O'Brien as the magnificently drunken and eloquent newspaper editor, Dutton Peabody.

Dir: John Ford; **Prod**: Willis Goldbeck; **Scr**: James Warner Bellah, Willis Goldbeck; **DOP**: William C. Clothier; **Score**: Cyril Mockridge.

(*Opposite page*) Tom Doniphon (John Wayne) gives Hallie (Vera Miles) a cactus rose in *The Man Who Shot Liberty Valance*. On the left, Ranse (James Stewart) and Pompey (Woody Strode), on the right Ericson (John Qualen) and Mrs Ericson (Jeanette Nolan)

McCabe and Mrs Miller
US, 1971 – 120 mins
Robert Altman

Accompanied throughout by the plaintive songs of Leonard Cohen, this is a bitter-sweet love story set in a ramshackle town in the mountains of the north-west. John McCabe (Warren Beatty) arrives in Presbyterian Church as a gambler and with a reputation as a gunfighter, though he claims to be merely a businessman. Sensing an opportunity, he buys three whores and sets them up to service the local miners. But the enterprise is squalidly run until the arrival of Mrs Miller (Julie Christie), a cockney prostitute who knows the brothel business inside out. She offers to run things for him, encouraging him to invest in lavish facilities ('You think small,' she admonishes McCabe). Before long they are making serious money, and the relationship between the two becomes tender, although Mrs Miller insists that McCabe pay her for his pleasure, like her other customers. Unknown to him, she is an opium smoker, which seems to explain her emotional reserve.

McCabe's success attracts the attention of a mining company, who send two representatives to buy him out. Puffed up with his new-found sense of achievement, McCabe turns their offer down flat, an act which ultimately leads to disaster. He is encouraged to resist the company's demands by a windbag of a lawyer (William Devane), but Mrs Miller has misgivings. When the company send the intimidating Butler (Hugh Millais) to scare McCabe into selling up, he finds himself on his own against three hardened killers. A protracted shootout in the snow ends in tragedy, while Mrs Miller lies in an opium haze, ignorant of McCabe's fate.

The story is told in Robert Altman's familiar style, with 'realistic' framing (objects and people intervening between the spectator and speaking characters) and his usual densely textured sound (overlapping conversations and half-heard throwaway remarks). The view of the west is relentlessly downbeat. It's always either raining or snowing, the town is a collection of lean-to shacks set amid a sea of mud, and the fate of the characters is recorded with a brutal lack of sentimentality. Shelley Duvall plays Ida, a mail-order bride who soon ends up in the whorehouse. Keith Carradine is a cheerful young cowboy who delightedly samples the brothel's wares and who is then arbitrarily shot dead by the Kid (Manfred Schulz), a cold-blooded little killer who accompanies Butler.

McCabe himself is a comic rather than a heroic figure, a boastful little boy forever trying to claim the credit for Mrs Miller's innovations, and acted by Beatty with considerable restraint and charm. Christie wonderfully communicates an underlying sadness beneath her common-sense manner. In some ways her character is a variation on the 'tart with a heart' theme so common in the Western, but she invests it with a mystery and depth. Ultimately it is this, rather than her addiction, which renders her unattainable. 'I've got poetry in me,' McCabe declaims to an empty room, but not enough, it seems, to pierce through her reserve.

Dir: Robert Altman; **Prod**: David Foster, Mitchell Brower; **Scr**: Robert Altman, Brian McKay; **DOP**: Vilmos Zsigmond; **Score**: Leonard Cohen.

The Missouri Breaks
US, 1976 – 126 mins
Arthur Penn

With an original screenplay by Thomas McGuane (who also wrote *Tom Horn* [1980] and *Rancho Deluxe* [1974]), this is one of the best Westerns of the 1970s. Set in Montana, it's a story which has much in common with *Heaven's Gate* (made four years later); though not based on historical characters, it has a similar foundation in the reality of the Johnson County War in Wyoming in the 1890s, when cattle barons hired gunmen to terrorise settlers they accused of rustling.

Braxton (John McLiam) is a wealthy rancher whose cultured taste in literature (he reads *Tristram Shandy*) does not conceal his ruthlessness in dealing with threats to his property. After hanging a suspected rustler he rails against the settlers coming into his locality, including 'failed grangers, half-breed Scandinavians' and others. When Braxton's foreman is himself hanged in revenge, Braxton decides to bring in a 'regulator', Robert E. Lee Clayton (Marlon Brando), despite his daughter's dislike of his methods. Meanwhile Tom Logan (Jack Nicholson), finding his trade of horse rustling becoming more difficult, tries train robbery instead, with farcical results. He and his gang revert to rustling and purchase a ranch next to Braxton's as a relay station. Logan starts an affair with Braxton's daughter Jane (Kathleen Lloyd), who is bored with life out west. Clayton suspects the truth about Logan and embarks on a campaign of murder against Logan and his gang. ('Regulator – ain't that like a dry-gulcher?' Logan had asked on being introduced.) Clayton drowns Little Tod (Randy Quaid), having failed to get information from him. Logan tries to get Clayton to draw on him but fails, and Clayton picks off the rest of the gang one by one, shooting one while he is having sex with a farmer's wife and another while he is taking a shit. Cal (Harry Dean Stanton) is despatched by means of a sharp iron spike, but eventually Logan gets to Clayton and cuts his throat. In a final confrontation Braxton tries to shoot Logan but is himself killed. Logan and Jane agree to meet when things have quietened down.

Brando gives one of his most eccentric performances, first spied riding underneath his horse, speaking in a broad Irish accent, complaining of toothache and telling Braxton not to feed him okra. Later he disguises himself in women's clothes, and spends time sitting on his horse watching birds through binoculars. But the violence is murderous and the tension between Clayton and Logan electric. Nicholson too is in fine form, 'slicker than snot on a door knob', as an associate remarks, irrigating his carefully tended cabbages while seducing the compliant Jane. Besides producing a clear-sighted analysis of class relations and economics, McGuane's dialogue is wonderfully oracular: 'He personified the American west in the days of its rowdy youth,' says one character of another.

Dir: Arthur Penn; **Prod**: Robert M. Sherman; **Scr**: Thomas McGuane; **DOP**: Michael Butler; **Score**: John Williams.

(*Next page*) *The Missouri Breaks*: Robert E. Lee Clayton (Marlon Brando) is accosted in the bath by Tom Logan (Jack Nicholson)

Monte Walsh
US, 1970 – 108 mins
William A. Fraker

Jack Schaefer is best known as the author of *Shane* (1949), but his *Monte Walsh* is an even better novel, and was turned into an equally pleasurable film. Lee Marvin and Jack Palance are admirably cast as the two ageing cowboys Monte and his friend Chet (Palance had played the entirely different role of the gunman Wilson in the film version of *Shane*). The first half of the film has no structured plot, being merely a series of vignettes illustrating the hard times experienced by cowboys after the disastrous winter of 1886–7. There is little work to be found, and although Monte and Chet are given jobs on the Slash Y ranch, the manager is at the mercy of the owners, now the Consolidated Cattle Co., contemptuously dismissed as a bunch of accountants. Eventually he has to lay off the three youngest cow-hands. One of them, Shorty (Mitch Ryan), is reduced to rustling. Chet decides there is no future in cowboying, though Monte disagrees ('It ain't dead if there's one cowboy taking care of one cow'). Chet moves into town and marries the widow of a hardware merchant. But when he refuses Shorty a loan he is shot dead. Monte, who has now also lost his job, goes in pursuit of Shorty.

Apart from isolated moments of violence, this is a gentle film, its moments of broad comedy not disguising its underlying sadness. Monte has an intermittent but long-standing relationship with Martine (Jeanne Moreau), the local whore, and there's a wonderful wordless scene where he visits her after a long absence and tries to roll a cigarette in bed while she is determined to initiate another bout of love-making. Periodically she cuts his hair, and when she finally dies Monte cuts a lock of her hair as a keepsake.

Monte is a romantic, desperately holding on to the only life he knows (when offered work he is adamant: 'I ain't doing anything I can't do from a horse'). Chet is more realistic: 'Nobody gets to be a cowboy for ever.' After Chet's marriage, Monte discusses the subject with

Martine, but concludes that 'Cowboys don't get married. Unless they stop being cowboys.' After a spectacular feat of riding on a half-tamed horse, during which he wrecks half the town, Monte is offered a job in a circus, dressed up as 'Texas Jack Butler'. But Monte finds the idea of caricaturing the west distasteful: 'I ain't spitting on my whole life.' In the last scene of the film, we find him repeating word for word the conversation he has with Chet in the opening scene, about a man who

Cowboy Monte Walsh (Lee Marvin) has to face the passing of time in the elegiac *Monte Walsh*

once wrestled with wolves. But this time Monte has no one left to talk to but his horse. The theme song of the film, 'The Good Times Are Coming', sung by Mama Cass, was a big hit, but its message here can only be ironic.

Dir: William A. Fraker; **Prod**: Hal Landers, Bobby Roberts; **Scr**: David Zelag Goodman, Lukas Heller; **DOP**: David M. Walsh; **Score**: John Barry.

My Darling Clementine
US, 1946 – 96 mins
John Ford

Henry Fonda had already played a couple of saintly heroes (Abraham Lincoln, Tom Joad) for John Ford before being cast as Wyatt Earp. Despite Ford's claim that he knew Earp and 'So in *My Darling Clementine* we did it exactly the way it had been', the film is basically a hagiography of a man who in truth was a ruthless opportunist. But this matters little; the charm and delicacy of Ford's vision outweigh any historical liberties. At the beginning, arriving in Tombstone with his brothers, Wyatt is merely irritated by the general lawlessness disturbing his ritual visit to the barber's, which marks his passage from the wilderness to civilisation. But once his young brother James is murdered by the evil Clantons, Wyatt commits himself to the cause of law and order. In this he makes an uneasy alliance with Doc Holliday (Victor Mature), a consumptive gambler drinking himself to death. Doc is pursued by two women, the half-Indian Chihuahua (Linda Darnell), sultry and inconstant, and the virginal Clementine (Cathy Downs), who has come from the east to rescue him from his self-disgust.

Gradually Tombstone is transformed into an island of civilisation in the wilderness, the latter symbolised by the towers of Monument Valley which encircle the collection of frame buildings. A Shakespearean actor visits town, and when, after being rescued from the unruly audience by Earp and Holliday, he dries in his recitation of Hamlet's 'To be or not to be' speech, Holliday, a man of culture despite his frequentation of saloons, completes the soliloquy. In a justly famous scene, Wyatt is induced to accompany Clementine to the first service being held in the half-built church, where the kindly preacher (Russell Simpson) invites the congregation to a 'dag-blasted good dance', always an affirmation of community in the Fordian universe. Earp's stiffness on the dance floor contrasts with Clementine's grace and is an indication that though he is the agent of civilisation, he is far from the finished article himself, and retains a rough manliness necessary for enforcing the law.

But old man Clanton (Walter Brennan) stands in the way of Earp's mission. Eventually a confrontation becomes inevitable, the two sides meeting at dawn at the O.K. Corral. In a carefully orchestrated sequence of manoeuvring, Earp and his allies prevail, but not before Holliday has been gunned down. (In fact Holliday died six years later, of TB.) At the end of the film Wyatt takes his leave of Tombstone and Clementine, but promises to return.

Darryl Zanuck, a notoriously hands-on studio chief, was dissatisfied with Ford's edit of the film. He set about trimming approximately half an hour, as well as adding extra music. He professed to like Ford's original ending, in which Wyatt, leaving Tombstone to visit his father in California, shyly shakes Clementine by the hand, but claimed that preview audiences could not understand such restraint. Zanuck called Fonda and Downs back for re-shoots, and added an embrace. Fortunately, something like Ford's original has now been discovered, and both this and the studio's version are now available on DVD, with a helpful commentary on the differences.

Dir: John Ford; **Prod**: Samuel G. Engel; **Scr**: Winston Miller, Samuel G. Engel; **DOP**: Joseph MacDonald; **Score**: Cyril Mockridge.

(*Opposite page*) Wyatt Earp (Henry Fonda) at ease on the main street of Tombstone in *My Darling Clementine*

The Naked Spur
US, 1952 – 91 mins
Anthony Mann

Shot almost entirely on location in the Rocky Mountains of Colorado, this is Anthony Mann's most pared-down, elemental Western, with only five characters appearing on screen, except for some anonymous Indians. Howard Kemp (James Stewart) is pursuing Ben Vandergroat (Robert Ryan), wanted for murder in Kansas. He runs into Jesse Tate (Millard Mitchell), an old-timer prospecting for gold, who offers to help him in exchange for payment. Before they can capture Ben, Anderson (Ralph Meeker), a discharged army officer, arrives on the scene, and together the three men overcome Ben, though not before some spirited resistance by Lina (Janet Leigh), the daughter of his former partner in crime.

Kemp is shame-faced when it emerges that there is a $5,000 reward for Ben, dead or alive. Jesse and Anderson both want a share of the money. Meanwhile Ben sets about sowing seeds of discord among his three captors, suggesting that each of them has an interest in seeing the others dead: 'Money splits better two ways than three.' It becomes evident that Ben has known Kemp previously and finally the story comes out that, before going away to the Civil War, Kemp gifted his ranch to his girlfriend, but she sold it and went off with another man. He wants the reward money to buy it back. Ben taunts him continually for his failure: 'Choosing a way to die, what's the difference? Choosing a way to live, that's the hard part.'

In the woods they come across some Blackfoot Indians, who are pursuing Anderson for a wrong he did them. Anderson provokes a shootout, the Indians are rebuffed but Kemp is shot in the leg. Ben makes several attempts to escape, but Lina gradually comes to see the evil in him. At last Ben talks Jesse into helping him get away, in exchange for the location of a gold mine he claims to have discovered. When he shoots Jesse in cold blood, Lina is outraged and foils his attempt to ambush Kemp and Anderson. Ben is shot and his body falls into a flooded river, Anderson tries to pull him out, desperate to get the reward, but is swept away. Kemp finally leaves Ben's body and his past behind, and offers to take Lina to California.

As so often in Mann's Westerns, the hero undergoes a calvary of both physical and mental torment before at last finding salvation. Kemp spends almost the entire film in agony from his leg wound, and in addition is beaten, falls down a cliff and is pushed off his horse. Worse, he is humiliated by Ben's knowledge of his past.

Meeker and Ryan make excellent foils, equally unscrupulous, smiling all the time while plotting murder. But the landscape is as much a character as they. Twice Kemp has to make a perilous climb up a cliff-face, and rocks and raging torrents are as much an obstacle as his companions. At the end, Mann tilts the camera upwards, signifying that Kemp has overcome all.

Dir: Anthony Mann; **Prod**: William H. Wright; **Scr**: Sam Rolfe, Harold Jack Bloom; **DOP**: William C. Mellor; **Score**: Bronislau Kaper.

Oh, Susanna!
US, 1936 – 59 mins
Joseph Kane

While the A-feature Western languished during the 1930s, until revived
at the end of the decade by *Stagecoach* and some other successes,
production of B-feature and series Westerns boomed, from both the
major studios and the smaller Poverty Row outfits. A major contribution
came from the new breed of singing cowboys, made possible by the
introduction of sound into the cinema, and motivated by the increasing
popularity of radio. Chief among these was Gene Autry, who topped the
specialist Western stars poll in *Motion Picture Herald* from 1937 until
called into the army in 1943, when he was replaced by Roy Rogers.

The format in Autry's pictures did not vary much. Gene invariably
plays himself, singing star Gene Autry. The setting is a never-never-land
somewhere out west at a time which though recognisably part of the
present, in which motor cars, phonograph records and radios are among
the trappings of everyday life, people dress in Western clothes and
habitually ride horses. There is always comedy, usually supplied by
Autry's regular sidekick Smiley Burnette, there will be a girl but little
overt love-making, and Gene will sing several Western ballads in his light,
musical voice.

In *Oh, Susanna!*, Gene is on his way by train to see an old friend to
whom he has lent money to develop his dude ranch. He is attacked by
Wolf Benson (Boothe Howard), an escaped murderer, who assumes his
identity and tosses Gene from the train. Rescued by Frog Millhouse
(Smiley Burnette) and Professor Daniels (Earle Hodgkins), who have a
travelling minstrel show, Gene is arrested as the murderer in Sage City.
Frog and the professor secure his release by persuading the judge that
Gene prove his identity by singing. Gene's throat has been hurt in the
struggle to arrest him, so his two friends fix up a phonograph recording
outside the jailhouse window and Gene mimes a song. But the ruse of
the phonograph is discovered by the sheriff and Gene is still on the run.

Under the alias of Tex Smith he checks in to the dude ranch and gives a singing performance, as well as eventually thwarting Benson's plans to steal the valuables of the guests.

Significantly, it's Gene's voice rather than his physical appearance that authenticates his identity, thus confirming in the narrative his status as a singing star. When first called upon to prove who he is, the audience assembled to hear him sing consists mainly of elderly rubes, but later when he performs at the dude ranch he entertains a group of prosperous middle-class guests, thus demonstrating the breadth of his appeal. Autry's popularity with the female audience gives the lie to assertions that Westerns attracted an exclusively male audience and the action sequences, the fights and chases, are relatively perfunctory. On the other hand, Autry's embrace of his singing partner at the end of the film comes as a bit of a shock given that they have scarcely had a scene together; evidently too much love-making might lose the male audience.

Dir: Joseph Kane; **Prod:** Nat Levine; **Scr:** Oliver Drake; **DOP:** William Nobles; **Score:** Gene Autry, Smiley Burnette, Oliver Drake, Sam H. Stept.

Once Upon a Time in the West/ C'era una volta il west
Italy/USA, 1968 – 159 mins
Sergio Leone

Leone's masterpiece is the culmination of his distinctive contribution to the Western genre. In Leone's west, characters are driven by revenge, greed or lust, but never by a sense of community or the desire to civilise the wilderness. For the director it's an opportunity to pursue aesthetic, not social ends. Indeed, *Once Upon a Time* is more about other Western movies than it is about the west itself. It begins with an elaborate parody of *High Noon* (1952), as three heavies wait at a train station. Two of them, Woody Strode and Jack Elam, are familiar faces from the Hollywood Western, and when the train at last arrives it deposits another recognisable figure, Charles Bronson, in the role of Harmonica. The following scene, which has echoes of *Shane* (1953) as a little boy mimes shooting at birds, contains a real shock. The saintly Henry Fonda, veteran of such Ford Westerns as *My Darling Clementine* (1946), appears as Frank, a heartless killer who despatches the McBain family, father and three children. And in the third scene, the heroine of the film, Jill McBain (Claudia Cardinale) arrives in Flagstone expecting to meet her new husband, McBain. Disappointed at his non-arrival, she hires a buggy and is driven out into the desert, emerging into none other than the holy of holies, John Ford's Monument Valley, as Ennio Morricone's operatic music swells irresistibly on the soundtrack.

Two mysteries sustain the narrative of the film: why is Harmonica on the track of Frank, and why did McBain build his house out in the desert? The railroad connects the questions. Frank is working for Morton (Gabriele Ferzetti), the crippled head of the railroad company, who wants McBain off his land because it contains the only water for fifty miles west of Flagstone. Jill is befriended both by Harmonica and by Cheyenne (Jason Robards), a bandit wrongly suspected of McBain's murder. At the end Harmonica obtains his revenge, but both men finally leave Jill to her now-assured prosperity, as the railroad pushes through her land.

Severely truncated on its American release, the film did poorly at the box office compared to Leone's previous Westerns. But its reputation has climbed ever since. The sometimes tortoise-like pace of the narrative needs to be set against the originality of Leone's conceptions and the stylistic bravura. Morton is a sinister creation, eaten up with TB, as he explains his philosophy to Frank ('There are many kinds of weapons and the only one that can stop that [a gun] is this [a wad of money]'). In fact money does not save him, and he dies in a puddle, the closest he gets to his dream of reaching the waters of the Pacific. The film is full of deft and amusing touches, as when Cheyenne holds his boot outside over the window of a railroad car, hypnotising an unsuspecting victim before shooting him with a gun hidden in the toe. But it's also a film on a grand scale; for once, the term epic does not seem undeserved.

Dir: Sergio Leone; **Prod**: Fulvio Morsella; **Scr**: Sergio Leone, Sergio Donati; **DOP**: Tonino Delli Colli; **Score**: Ennio Morricone.

(*Next page*) Henry Fonda as the evil Frank, an unaccustomed role in *Once Upon a Time in the West*

One-Eyed Jacks
US, 1960 – 137 mins
Marlon Brando

One-Eyed Jacks has an interesting pedigree. Before he had directed any feature films, Sam Peckinpah came across a novel by Charles Neider, first published in 1956. It was a fictionalised version of the story of Billy the Kid. Peckinpah's script of the novel was shown to Marlon Brando, who optioned the book, and suggested an up-and-coming director, Stanley Kubrick, should be hired to shoot it. But Brando and Kubrick fell out, and Brando then hired a succession of writers to make substantial changes to Peckinpah's script, including the substitution of a happy ending. Eventually, Brando decided to direct the film himself, his only venture behind the camera.

Brando, named Rio but usually called just 'Kid', is first glimpsed down in Mexico, sitting on the counter of a bank he is robbing, calmly eating a banana. Roguishly he chides a woman bank customer for trying to hide a ring, which he steals and later presents to a high-class Mexican lady, insisting it belonged to his mother. But the Kid is himself deceived when his partner in crime, Dad Longworth (Karl Malden), fails to come back for him when the Kid is surrounded by Federales. After five years in a Mexican jail, the Kid goes in search of Longworth, who by now is sheriff of a small town on the Monterey peninsula in California and has a wife (Katy Jurado) and teenage stepdaughter Louisa (Pina Pellicer). The Kid, together with the surly Bob Amory (Ben Johnson), plans to rob the bank while exacting revenge on Longworth. But after the Kid kills a man in a saloon, Longworth, suspicious of the Kid's intentions and knowing that Louisa has fallen in love with him, savagely whips the Kid in public and crushes his gun-hand (a scene not present in the original novel).

Eventually the Kid recovers and he and his companions attempt to rob the bank. But things go wrong; a bystander is killed and the Kid is locked up in jail, waiting to be hanged, with Longworth's sadistic deputy Lon Dedrick (Slim Pickens) gloating over his fate. Finally, the Kid makes a daring escape, shoots Longworth and rides off after promising Louisa he will return.

As usual, Brando turns in a charismatic performance, by turns charming and full of menace. Malden too is excellent as the Pat Garrett figure, Longworth, hiding cunning and vindictive anger under his respectable exterior, the soubriquet Dad serving to point up the oedipal subtext. Besides the basic relationship of the Kid and his mentor/nemesis, other aspects of the traditional Billy the Kid narrative remain, such as the escape from jail, repeated in Peckinpah's later treatment of the story, *Pat*

Marlon Brando as Rio being whipped by Sheriff Longworth (Karl Malden) in *One-Eyed Jacks*

Garrett and Billy the Kid (1973). But there is much that is strikingly original in Brando's version, including the use of the California coast as a location, almost uniquely in the Western. Day after day the Kid practises his shooting with his damaged hand, against a backdrop of crashing surf and pristine yellow sands. Only the brutish Amory (an unusually unsympathetic performance by Fordian stalwart Ben Johnson) cannot appreciate the scene, grousing about 'them damn waves flopping in all day'.

The significance of the title is obscure, though it has been suggested there is an obscene implication.

Dir: Marlon Brando; **Prod**: Frank P. Rosenberg; **Scr**: Guy Trosper, Calder Willingham; **DOP**: Charles B. Lang Jr; **Score**: Hugo Friedhofer.

Open Range
US, 2004 – 138 mins
Kevin Costner

With his appearances in *Silverado* (1985) and *Wyatt Earp* (1994), and his
direction of himself in *Dances With Wolves* (1990), Kevin Costner may be
running a single-handed campaign to save the Western from oblivion.
Eschewing any attempt at a revisionist view, *Open Range* is resolutely
traditional, combining elements of the range-war scenario with the
town-tamer plot. Boss Spearman (Robert Duvall) is an ageing cowboy
running cattle on the open range with the help of Charlie Waite (Kevin
Costner), a Civil War veteran, Button (Diego Luna), a youthful Latino and
Mose (Abraham Benrubi), an amiable giant. When Mose is arrested in
the nearby town, Boss and Charlie go to rescue him, only to be warned
off the range by Baxter (Michael Gambon), a bullying rancher who has
the town in his pocket and who declares that the days of free range are
over. Later, while Boss and Charlie are absent, Baxter's men attack their
camp, killing Mose and wounding Button. Having already made the
acquaintance of Sue (Annette Bening), the sister of the town doctor, they
take Button to her for treatment. Their feud with Baxter and Poole
(James Russo), the sheriff he employs, escalates. Having imprisoned the
sheriff in his own jail, Charlie and Boss wait for the inevitable
confrontation with Baxter, after Charlie has shyly made known to Sue his
feelings for her.

Much in the story is familiar. Baxter is in the mould of previously
dictatorial cattle barons like Ryker in *Shane* (1953), while the youthful
Button is the latest in a long line of young men in the Western who get
taken in hand by their elders and betters. Charlie is, like many before
him, trying to live down the trauma of the Civil War and attempting to
leave behind a violent past which keeps catching up with him. He offers
a rationale for his behaviour that would find an echo in many other
Westerns: 'You may not know this, but there's things gnaw at a man
worse than dying.' The central relationship of the film, as so often in the

Western, is between two men, their mutual respect ripening into love. Boss himself is well aware of this, remarking to Sue that he and Charlie are like a married couple, always bickering but with underlying affection.

What makes this such a successful film, however, is not so much its deployment of traditional elements but its sensitivity and insight, as well as its beauty. There are some stunning views of sweeping landscapes and lovely shots of horses, contrasting with the squalor of the town. There are deft and surprising touches, such as Charlie and Boss eating chocolate before the big showdown, or drinking tea with Sue, unable to get their fingers into the dainty cup handles. Costner's performance gives Charlie the right combination of shyness and capacity for violence. Duvall is perfect as Boss, kindly towards Button and Mose, with a sly sense of humour, but implacable towards those who would try to bully him. Annette Bening makes the most of that unusual thing in a Hollywood film, a romantic part for a woman over forty.

Dir: Kevin Costner; **Prod**: David Valdes, Kevin Costner, Jake Eberts; **Scr**: Craig Storper; **DOP**: James Muro; **Score**: Michael Kamen.

The Outlaw Josey Wales
US, 1976 – 134 mins
Clint Eastwood

Together with *Unforgiven* (1992), this is Eastwood's best achievement in
the genre, but *The Outlaw Josey Wales* had a difficult birth. Originally
assigned to director Phil Kaufman and produced by Eastwood's own
Malpaso company, the star and director fell out, largely over Kaufman's
shooting style, which was more leisurely than Eastwood liked. Eastwood
took over direction, as well as playing the lead role of Josey. The film
begins with Josey ploughing his land on the Kansas–Missouri border
during the Civil War. Northern guerrillas ('Redlegs') murder his family.
Josey joins the Confederates, fighting under the leadership of Fletcher
(John Vernon), but when Fletcher tries to surrender at the war's end
Josey narrowly survives a massacre. Fleeing south to Texas, he is pursued
by the vindictive Redleg commander Terrill (Bill McKinney). As he
wanders deeper into the wilderness he acquires a series of travelling
companions. First is Lone Watie (Chief Dan George), an elderly Indian
with a wry sense of humour. Josey rescues Little Moonlight (Geraldine
Keams) from her brutal white captor and then saves Laura Lee (Sondra
Locke) from being raped by Comancheros. Together with Laura's
grandmother and a stray dog, the little band finally arrive at a ranch the
white women have inherited. It stands on Indian land and a
confrontation appears inevitable, but Josey persuades the Comanche
chief Ten Bears (Will Sampson) that co-existence is possible. Once Josey
has despatched Terrill, the little band may live in peace.

It's essentially a film of reconciliation, offering, without forcing the
point, some parallels between the Civil War and the Vietnam War in the
year of the bicentenary ('I guess we all died a little in that damned war,'
Josey says). The character Eastwood plays marks a development from the
cynical loner, the Man with No Name, that Eastwood played in his Italian
Westerns. Traumatised, Josey is reluctant to become involved in new
personal commitments, yet as he journeys he acquires piece by piece a

substitute family for the one he has lost. Bruce Surtees' photography makes the most of the widely varied landscapes but in the more intimate moments there's a striking use of shade and even darkness that was to become an Eastwood trademark.

The original novel on which the film was based is credited to Forrest Carter, who claimed to be part-Cherokee. Only after the film came out was it revealed that the author was in fact Asa Carter, a white supremacist, an anti-Semite and a speech-writer for George Wallace, the notorious segregationist governor of Alabama. Carter seems to have persuaded himself by some tortuous mental process that despite his virulent pro-white views, the Indians of the south such as the Cherokee, who were removed from their ancestral lands in the 1830s, had much in common with white southerners, dispossessed and exploited by the north after defeat in the Civil War. However, this theme does not survive into the film which, though sympathetic to the south as many Westerns are, has more conventionally liberal sentiments towards the Indians.

Dir: Clint Eastwood; **Prod**: Robert Daley; **Scr**: Phil Kaufman, Sonia Chernus; **DOP**: Bruce Surtees; **Score**: Jerry Fielding.

The Paleface
US, 1948 – 91 mins
Norman Z. McLeod

As in most comedy Westerns, it's the concept of masculinity, the idea
that 'a man's gotta do what a man's gotta do', that is the occasion of
most of the humour in *The Paleface*. Frank Tashlin's screenplay, in
partnership with Edmund L. Hartmann, combines some typically Tashlin
visual jokes ('the dawn broke' – the letters on the screen break up and
fall away) with plenty of verbal gags for Bob Hope to sink his teeth into.
Hope projects onto the role of Painless Potter, travelling dentist, his usual
screen persona: lecherous, venal, cowardly and opportunistic. The
improbable plot has Jane Russell as Calamity Jane being offered a free
pardon by the authorities for some unspecified crime if she will help
track down a group of crooks who are running guns to the Indians. The
scheme is for her to join a wagon train going west, but her fellow agent
is killed and she needs a new partner to preserve her cover. Potter has
been run out of town by an irate patient and, much to his delight,
Calamity proposes marriage. His increasingly desperate attempts to
consummate this marriage of convenience form one of the running gags
of the film.

When they are attacked by Indians, Calamity shoots them all, but it
looks as if Potter, hiding in a barrel, has performed the deed. He is hailed
as a hero ('You've got the courage of a lion!' 'Oh, it's nothing, brave men
run in our family,' quips Potter). Believing his own myth, Potter swaps his
dentist's dudes for a cowboy outfit and swaggers about in a hilarious
parody of Western machismo, attempting and abysmally failing to roll a
cigarette one-handed. Having given the local badman till sundown to get
out of town, Potter stalks the main street, getting increasingly confused
over the mass of advice he has been given about watching out for wind
speed, his opponent's shooting habits and other variables. When it comes
to the confrontation, Calamity again intervenes, in the manner of John
Wayne in *The Man Who Shot Liberty Valance* (1962).

Hidden in an undertaker's parlour waiting to find out when the bad guys will come and collect a shipment of dynamite, Potter and Calamity are captured by the Indians. Potter escapes, then deliberates whether to return to rescue his wife. Torn between courage and cowardice he protests: 'I'm not a mouse, I'm not a man. I'm a dentist.' Recaptured, he is tied to a stake by three of the most celebrated actors in Indian roles: Chief Yowlachie, born on the Yakima reservation in Washington State, Henry Brandon, born in Berlin as Heinrich von Kleinbach, who also played Scar in *The Searchers* (1956), and Iron Eyes Cody, who spent a lifetime masquerading as a genuine Native American but who was born the child of Italian immigrants in Louisiana.

Four years later Hope and Russell were joined by Roy Rogers for a sequel, *Son of Paleface*, which is if anything funnier than the original.

Dir: Norman Z. McLeod; **Prod**: Robert L. Welch; **Scr**: Edmund L. Hartmann, Frank Tashlin; **DOP**: Ray Rennahan; **Score**: Victor Young, Ray Evans, Jay Livingston.

Pale Rider
US, 1985 – 116 mins
Clint Eastwood

Eastwood's Westerns often have the happy knack of drawing on the
genre's roots while giving a new twist to a traditional form. *Pale Rider*
owes an obvious debt to *Shane* (1953), made thirty years previously. As
in the earlier film, a mysterious gunfighter emerges out of nowhere to
assist a group of honest workers against a rich and powerful oppressor.
The film opens with a spectacular action scene, as a body of riders
thunder across the landscape and ride through a mining camp, wrecking
it and beating the occupants. This is instigated by LaHood (Richard
Dysart), who covets the claim which the independent miners are working
on. As in *Shane*, the film opposes a kind of feudal despotism to the more
democratic nature of the modest farmers or miners. Similar to *Shane* also
is the hero's relationship with someone much younger, who is the first to
set eyes on him. In this case, the Preacher (Eastwood) is first glimpsed by
Megan (Sydney Penny), a fourteen-year old girl. As he rides into view,
she is reading her Bible, from the book of Revelation: 'And I looked and
beheld a pale horse and his name that sat on him was Death, and Hell
followed with him.'

The Preacher has an air of mystery, and as the film progresses we
become aware that he has supernatural qualities, having apparently
come back from the dead after being shot in the back (rather in the
manner of Eastwood's earlier *High Plains Drifter* [1972]). He throws in his
lot with the small miners, who are not only more democratic but also
ecologically superior, working their claims with pick and shovel, whereas
LaHood employs a hydraulic system that literally washes away the
landscape. The Preacher assists Hull Barret (Michael Moriarty), one of the
miners, when he is being beaten by LaHood's hired thugs, in a scene
similar to that in which Shane fights by the side of Joe, and later the
Preacher helps remove a huge boulder blocking the diggings, as Shane
had helped Joe shift a tree trunk on his farm. Both Megan and her

mother Sarah (Carrie Snodgrass) are attracted to the Preacher; while he gently tells Megan she is too young, he sleeps with Sarah, despite the fact that she has a relationship with Barret, thus making manifest the sexual relationship which in *Shane* was only latent.

The final shootout between a solitary Preacher and the gang of hired guns assembled by Sheriff Stockburn (John Russell), all of them clad in long brown dusters, is memorably staged, with the Preacher appearing almost magically in doorways and alley-ways as he methodically guns down every one. Shot in the majestic setting of the Sawtooth Range in Idaho, this is a good-looking film, though the interiors are as darkly brooding as anything in Eastwood's oeuvre. Perhaps to some the mystical overtones will seem unconvincing, but the film was one of the star's most successful at the box office.

Dir: Clint Eastwood; **Prod**: Fritz Manes; **Scr**: Michael Butler, Dennis Shryack; **DOP**: Bruce Surtees; **Score**: Lennie Niehaus.

Pat Garrett and Billy the Kid
US, 1973 – 106 mins
Sam Peckinpah

This is Sam Peckinpah's last Western, and though its rambling structure and occasional incoherence show signs of decline (as well as being evidence of the studio interference from which the director so often suffered), it nevertheless contains some of the best things he ever did. Truncated on its first release, the film has now been put back to something like what Peckinpah intended, opening with a prologue showing the squalid death of Sheriff Pat Garrett (James Coburn), shot in the back in 1908. This is intercut with a scene of Billy the Kid (Kris Kristofferson) and his cronies thirty years earlier, killing time by engaging in target practice on some chickens. A key scene follows, in which Garrett explains why he has come to see Billy. The people who control New Mexico, the Santa Fe Ring, want law and order established at any cost in order to protect their investments. Billy accuses Pat of selling out. 'How does it feel?' he asks. 'It feels like times have changed,' Garrett answers. 'Times maybe, not me,' Billy replies. Refusing Garrett's advice to leave the territory, Billy is captured and imprisoned. Abused by the sadistic Ollinger (R. G. Armstrong), Billy makes a daring escape, killing Ollinger in the process. Billy and Garrett now play cat-and-mouse, Billy killing some of those who are trying to catch him, while Garrett in turn kills several of Billy's associates. Finally Garrett tracks him down to Fort Sumner, where Billy is in bed with his girlfriend, and shoots him dead.

Described by Jim Kitses as 'a drifting death-poem', the film has a strongly elegiac feel as it moves towards Billy's inevitable fate. At times it touches tragedy, as in the moving scene of the death of Sheriff Baker (Slim Pickens), played out to the music of Bob Dylan's 'Knocking at Heaven's Door' as he sits gunshot by the riverside. Dylan has a part in the film, though it's never very clear what his function in the plot is. Alongside him is a rich gallery of supporting players, including Katy Jurado, Chill Wills, Richard Jaeckel, Dub Taylor, Jack Elam, Harry Dean

Stanton, Barry Sullivan, Jason Robards and Emilio Fernandez, many of them veterans of previous Peckinpah films. Peckinpah even gave himself a part, as an undertaker.

Loosely based on the historical facts, the film emphasises the brutality of the west and the greed and power that lay beneath it, yet its ultimate effect is melancholic. Rather than being an exposé of the myth of the west, this is a film in which the characters enjoy posing, endlessly

The end of *Pat Garrett and Billy the Kid*: Billy (Kris Kristofferson) meets his nemesis, Garrett (James Coburn)

re-telling stories from the past. As Billy wanders aimlessly, Garrett feels increasing contempt for the people he is working for, and more and more self-disgust, his corruption expressed in a scene where he is bathed by a group of whores and confirmed when, after killing Billy, he frenziedly shoots at a mirror image of himself. Whereas Garrett is all cynicism, Billy is seen as youthfully naive, a Christ-like figure destined to be sacrificed.

Dir: Sam Peckinpah; **Prod**: Gordon Carroll; **Scr**: Rudolph Wurlitzer; **DOP**: John Coquillon; **Score**: Bob Dylan.

Pursued
US, 1947 – 101 mins
Raoul Walsh

Pursued begins in a ruined old ranch in the wilds of New Mexico at the
end of the nineteenth century, where Jeb Rand (Robert Mitchum) and
Thorley Callum (Teresa Wright) have taken refuge from their pursuers.
'Why did everything go wrong?' asks Thorley as they review their lives in
an extended flashback. The post-World War II period was the heyday of
film noir, and *Pursued* is a fascinating example of a noir Western,
borrowing a range of leitmotifs and stylistic tropes typical of the other
genre. Besides the extended flashback, and further flashbacks within it,
much of the film is literally noir, taking place at night, allowing full rein
for James Wong Howe's lustrous black-and-white photography, with
brilliant use of key lights and shadow. Thorley herself is a kind of *femme
fatale*, whose relationship with Jeb is a love–hate affair; she tells her
mother that she is marrying Jeb only in order to kill him. In true noir
fashion, Jeb and Thorley's lives are blighted by a tragic past they only
dimly perceive. The secret is contained in a childhood memory that dogs
Jeb throughout his life, in which a pair of boots with flashing spurs
march this way and that, a scene which led the film to become a prime
case study in the psychoanalytic readings of cinema that once dominated
Film Studies.

Over the course of the film we learn that Jeb's father has been killed
(the flashing spurs are his) and that Thorley's mother, Ma Callum (Judith
Anderson) has taken Jeb into her home, to be brought up with Thorley
and her brother Adam (John Rodney). As they grow up there is rivalry
between the two boys. When they are adults, war is declared with Spain
and one of the boys must go to fight. Jeb invites Thorley to toss a coin to
see who should go, and Jeb is selected. When he comes back a hero,
Adam's resentment is plain. Later, when Adam draws a gun on him, Jeb
is forced to shoot him. Thorley and her mother turn against him ('If I
were a man, I would have killed him long ago,' says Thorley). On her

wedding night, she draws a pistol, but Jeb hands her his own gun. She cannot shoot; instead, they embrace. Ma Callum's brother, Grant (Dean Jagger), has long been seeking Jeb's death, and at last the mystery is revealed: Ma Callum had dishonoured the Callums through an illicit relationship with Jeb's father, who was killed by Grant. At the ruined ranch at Bear Paw Butte, Jeb waits with Thorley for Grant to come. Surrounded, he gives himself up and is about to be hanged by Grant when Ma Callum shoots her brother and is reunited with Jeb and Thorley.

Perhaps the nearest thing in literature to *Pursued* is *Wuthering Heights*, with a similarly fateful passion. The emotion generated by the melodrama is whipped up to a frenzy by Max Steiner's wonderful score. The screenwriter, Niven Busch (married to Teresa Wright), was also the author of the novels, *Duel in the Sun* and *The Furies*, from which two equally delirious Westerns were made.

Dir: Raoul Walsh; **Prod**: Milton Sperling; **Scr**. Niven Busch; **DOP**: James Wong Howe; **Score**: Max Steiner.

Ramrod
US, 1947 – 94 mins
André de Toth

Brought to England from his native Hungary by fellow-countryman
Alexander Korda, André de Toth went to Hollywood in 1943 and, like
some other foreign-born directors such as Jacques Tourneur and Fritz
Lang, did some of his best work in the Western, the most American of
genres. *Ramrod* is an admirable example of the kind of small-scale,
ostensibly formulaic Western which brings out the best in all concerned.
The always-dependable Joel McCrea is Dave Nash, a cowboy who has
been driven to drink by personal tragedy, having lost both his wife and
small son. Rose (Arleen Whelan) comforts him, though Dave believes she
is in love with his friend Bill (Don DeFore). Connie Dickason (Veronica
Lake) is the daughter of a local rancher, who wishes her to marry Frank
Ivey (Preston Foster), the biggest cattle baron in the valley. Connie,
headstrong and stubborn, intends instead to marry Walt (Ian MacDonald),
who is going to stock his land with sheep. When Ivey warns this will lead
to violence, Walt deserts Connie. She decides to run his ranch herself and
hires Dave. Initially Dave says they must follow the law in standing up
against Ivey, but Connie is impatient. Using her physical attractions she
persuades Bill to stampede her herd and then puts the blame on Ivey.
When Sheriff Jim Crew (Donald Crisp), Dave's friend, goes to arrest Ivey,
he is shot and killed. Dave then decides to play rough and shoots one of
Ivey's men, but is himself wounded. Meanwhile Rose, who sees through
Connie, tells her that she is motivated by nothing but revenge and the
lust for power, and cares nothing for Dave: 'You're letting him break
himself on your greed and ambition.' On the run from Ivey's men, Dave
discovers the truth about Connie. With his arm in a sling he goes into
town and guns Ivey down in a shootout. Connie tells him of her plans for
the both of them, but Dave rejects her and goes to Rose instead.

Veronica Lake (who was married to director de Toth at the time) is
the undoubted star of the film as a blonde *femme fatale*, one moment

all simpering smiles as she makes up to whichever man she has most need of, the next moment screaming defiance at her father or trading withering insults with Frank Ivey. By contrast, the dark-haired Rose is worthy but dull. McCrea is also impressive, in a totally different style, as the gentle Dave, slow to anger but a man of principle while all around him are scheming. Even though wounded, there is never any doubt that he will finally be the man to stand up against the bullying Ivey, and the man to put him down. The final action sequences of the film are equally as striking as the dramatic interaction of the earlier part, as Ivey's men stalk both Dave and Bill through some impressive mountain scenery. But it is Connie we chiefly remember, lying in a cave by the firelight stroking the hair of the wounded Dave, looking like the cat that got the cream.

Dir: André de Toth; **Prod**: Harry Sherman; **Scr**: Jack Moffitt, Graham Baker, Cecile Kramer; **DOP**: Russell Harlan; **Score**: Adolph Deutsch.

Rancho Notorious
US, 1952 – 89 mins
Fritz Lang

Fritz Lang apparently had a great interest in the American west and liked to visit Indian reservations and go line-dancing. But this, the strangest of his three films in the genre, is a fantasy far removed from any reality. On the soundtrack a mournful ballad informs us that this is a story of 'hate, murder and revenge' and so it proves to be. Vern (Arthur Kennedy) finds his girlfriend raped and murdered. He sets off in pursuit of the man who did it and learns of a mysterious place called Chuckaluck and of the alluring Altar Keane (Marlene Dietrich) who runs it. Altar is first introduced taking part in a race with saloon girls, riding horseback on men as they crawl across the floor. A flashback shows Altar winning a fortune in a

Marlene Dietrich as Altar Keane gets ready to spin the Wheel of Fortune in *Rancho Notorious*

gambling saloon with the aid of Frenchy (Mel Ferrer), but now Frenchy is in jail, so Vern deliberately gets himself arrested in order to get close to him. The two escape and with Vern now a wanted man, Frenchy takes him to Chuckaluck, a ranch where Altar allows fugitives to hide out in exchange for a cut of their loot. Vern suspects one of them is the murderer he seeks, but he has no clue which. Vern and Altar are attracted to each other, though Frenchy tells Altar she will always be his: 'Time holds us together, and time's stronger than a rope.' Meanwhile Kinch (Lloyd Gough), the murderer of Vern's girlfriend, at last recognises Vern and plans to kill him during a bank hold-up that Frenchy has forced Vern to participate in. Vern escapes and journeys back alone to Chuckaluck to take Altar her share of the proceeds. A love scene begins to develop ('I like a woman who's sometimes cold as ice and sometimes burning like the sun,' he says). But then Vern recognises a piece of jewellery that belonged to his girlfriend. Altar says she bought it off Kinch. The scales fall from Vern's eyes and he is now disgusted with Altar's connivance in criminality. In a fast-moving climax, Vern seeks a confrontation with Kinch, and Altar decides to leave Chuckaluck for good, but in a final gun battle Kinch is killed and Altar dies as she stops a bullet meant for Frenchy.

The ballad which provides a running commentary on the action serves to highlight the stylised form of the film, which some have called 'Brechtian', and this is further emphasised by brightly coloured decor and some notably artificial 'exteriors', with south-west landscapes painted onto studio flats. Dietrich, who was over fifty when the film was made, has a suitably louche appearance for her *femme fatale* role and sings a couple of songs in her familiar throaty style. Kennedy is very good as an innocent caught up in a web of deceit, and Western stalwarts Jack Elam and Frank Ferguson (as a Bible-reading badman who reads over his victims) provide excellent support.

Dir: Fritz Lang; **Prod**: Howard Welsch; **Scr**: Daniel Taradash; **DOP**: Hal Mohr; **Score**: Emil Newman.

Red River
US, 1947 – 125 mins
Howard Hawks

'I didn't know the son of a bitch could act,' was John Ford's characteristically gruff compliment on John Wayne's performance in his first film for Howard Hawks. Journeying west across the plains Tom Dunson (Wayne), together with a boy, Matthew Garth (Mickey Kuhn), and his partner Groot (Walter Brennan), find some good cattle country in Texas and decide to settle. First they have to defend themselves against Indians, who, Dunson discovers, have wiped out the wagon train in which he has left his lover, and then stand up against the Mexican rancher who claims the land is his. In a chilling assertion of 'right is might' Dunson kills the rancher's hired gun and asserts his ownership. Years later, Matthew (now played by Montgomery Clift) is a grown man and Dunson's heir

Thomas Dunson (John Wayne) catches up with gambler Tess Millay (Joanne Dru) in *Red River*

apparent. After the end of the Civil War, with prices low in the south, Dunson decides to drive his cattle from Texas to the railhead in Kansas. Along the trail Dunson becomes increasingly dictatorial, believing that ruthlessness is the only way to impose his authority. He and Matthew disagree on his methods, and when Dunson tries to whip one of the trail-hands who is defying him, Matthew leads a rebellion, taking the herd away from Dunson and driving it on to Abilene. Dunson vows revenge.

Matthew meets up with Tess Millay (Joanne Dru), a professional cardsharp. During an attack by Indians, she is wounded in the shoulder by an arrow, and in a scene of barely suppressed eroticism Matthew sucks the poison from the wound. Matthew gets the herd to Abilene, where Dunson catches up with him. A fistfight ensues, but Tess breaks it up, forcing the two antagonists to admit to their mutual affection.

Though leavened by some typically Hawksian comedy (including a running gag about Groot's false teeth), the centre of the film is the intense, and increasingly bitter, oedipal battle between Dunson and the young man whom Dunson has chosen to ultimately replace him. Dunson's character is set at the start, when first he refuses to take his girl along with him on his detour into Texas, believing her presence will compromise him, and second, when he in effect murders in cold blood the Mexican who contests his claims to the land. But Wayne manages to make Dunson not only a towering presence but also a sympathetic figure, his faults resulting from his principles and his tenacity, taken to an extreme degree. It's a testament to Clift's acting talent that in his first starring role he was able to hold his own.

Borden Chase's script originally had Dunson dying at the end. The conclusion gave Hawks a lot of trouble, and he once admitted that what he shot was 'corny'. Everything in the film has prepared us for a final violent confrontation, but the fight between Dunson and Matthew turns out rather farcical, and Tess's intervention is neither plausible nor dramatically satisfying.

Dir: Howard Hawks; **Prod**: Howard Hawks; **Scr**: Borden Chase, Charles Schnee; **DOP**: Russell Harlan; **Score**: Dimitri Tiomkin.

Ride Lonesome
US, 1959 – 73 mins
Budd Boetticher

Together with *Comanche Station* (1960), this is the last fruit of the close
and productive relationship between director Budd Boetticher, writer Burt
Kennedy, producer Harry Joe Brown and star Randolph Scott. Like the
other film, it's shot in the Alabama Hills near Lone Pine in California, with
Mount Whitney in the background. As in all good Westerns, we see first
a rider in a landscape. It proves to be Ben Brigade (Scott), who is tracking
Billy John (James Best), wanted for murder. Brigade is intent on taking
him back to Santa Cruz. At a stagecoach station they encounter Boone
(Pernell Roberts) and his sidekick Whit (James Coburn), together with Mrs
Lane (Karen Steele), the wife of the station manager.

Brigade is a man of few words, nursing an inner sadness. Mrs Lane
thinks ill of him for being a bounty hunter, but he closes off discussion
with a curt 'You cook good coffee.' Later Boone waxes lyrical on Mrs
Lane's beauty, eliciting from Brigade only the grudging 'She ain't ugly.'
On the trail they encounter hostile Mescaleros, revealed in a supremely
elegant tracking shot with the five slowly riding through the desert as
the Indians appear in the distance. The Indians are fought off, but Mrs
Lane discovers that they have killed her husband. Boone then reveals to
her that he and Whit intend to take Billy John away from Brigade; they
themselves are wanted men, but can secure an amnesty if they deliver
him to the law. Brigade makes his position clear: 'I set out to take him to
Santa Cruz, and I full intend to do it.'

Andrew Sarris described Boetticher's Westerns as 'floating poker
games', and a battle of wits ensues as Brigade and Boone jockey for
position, the film alternating rides through the harsh landscape and quiet
moments by the campfire. Boone describes his wish to settle down and
informs the callow Whit that he will take him as a partner. White asks
why and is told, ''Cos I like you.' 'I never knew that,' Whit replies,
dumbfounded. Boone is sympathetic and engaging, but equally as

determined as Brigade. Asked by Mrs Lane why he must pursue the course he has chosen, he replies with a phrase first employed by the Scott character in *The Tall T* (1956): 'There's some things a man can't ride around.'

Brigade seems to be holding back rather than hastening to Santa Cruz, and at last explains why to Mrs Lane. He had been sheriff there and had put Billy John's brother Frank (Lee Van Cleef) in jail. Frank got

Ben Brigade (Randolph Scott) has a quiet campfire moment with Mrs Lane (Karen Steele) in *Ride Lonesome*

out and in revenge kidnapped Brigade's wife, then hanged her. When the party reach an isolated forked tree where the tragedy took place, Brigade waits for Frank to arrive, with Billy John's neck tied to the tree by a rope. The confrontation is rapidly resolved and, his revenge achieved, Brigade donates Billy John to Boone. As the two men and their captive ride away with Mrs Lane, they look back to see that Brigade has set the hanging tree on fire.

Dir: Budd Boetticher; **Prod**: Harry Joe Brown; **Scr**: Burt Kennedy; **DOP**: Charles Lawton Jr; **Score**: Heinz Roemheld.

Ride the High Country
US, 1962 – 98 mins
Sam Peckinpah

By the early 1960s the production of Westerns in Hollywood was in severe decline. Simultaneously, and perhaps the two things are related, there was a fashion for films about the end of the West. Among these, Peckinpah's *Ride the High Country* is one of the most poignant. Two ageing gunfighters, Steve and Gil, are recruited to escort a shipment of gold from the mines up in the mountains down to the bank. Both are down on their luck and looking for one last big job to help them settle down. But Gil, accompanied by a young man he has befriended, is embittered by the scant rewards he has got for a lifetime of service, and tries to take the gold for himself. Steve ties him up but Gil escapes, only to come to the rescue at the end when Steve is attacked by a gang of murderous brothers. In the ensuing gunfight the two stride out against superior odds and though the gang are defeated, Steve receives a mortal wound.

Steve and Gil are played by two veteran Western stars, Joel McCrea and Randolph Scott. The latter, giving one of his best performances, is cast against type. Instead of the grim-faced and stoical hero of Budd Boetticher's finest Westerns, Scott is all smooth-talking charm, disguising his criminal intentions though not his obvious affection for his old friend. McCrea is the personification of uncomplicated uprightness, trading biblical quotations with the oppressively religious farmer they meet along the trail.

The film has a brilliant opening sequence, with Steve riding into a small town on the Fourth of July to be confronted by various iconic objects signifying how the wild west era is closing: a motor car, a policeman in uniform and his old friend Gil dressed up as a Buffalo Bill-type showman, a walking pastiche of a Western hero. But once in the mountains, the film delivers in full value the traditional elements of the genre, as Steve and Gil find themselves protecting not only the gold but also Elsa (Mariette Hartley), a young girl who has foolishly allowed herself to marry one of a gang of brutish brothers. The ceremony, carried out in the mining camp's brothel by a drunken judge (memorably played by Edgar Buchanan), turns into a nightmarish gang rape, and Gil and Steve are obliged to rescue the girl and flee.

In an expertly acted film, several of the players went on to become regular fixtures in the Peckinpah repertory company, among them L. Q. Jones and Warren Oates as the most grotesque of the brothers, and R. G. Armstrong as the Bible-quoting fanatic. The final settling of scores takes place against the backdrop of golden aspen leaves in the Californian Sierras, a suitably elegiac landscape for a last stand. For both McCrea and Scott, this was their final Western and Steve's speech setting out his creed ('I want to enter my house justified') is a fitting epitaph for a long line of Western heroes.

Dir: Sam Peckinpah; **Prod**: Richard E. Lyons; **Scr**: N. B. Stone Jr; **DOP**: Lucien Ballard; **Score**: George Bassman.

Rio Bravo
US, 1959 – 141 mins
Howard Hawks

Rio Bravo is the pinnacle of Howard Hawks's art, containing one of John Wayne's very best performances while being a masterclass in ensemble acting. Wayne is John T. Chance, sheriff of a small south-western town who locks up the brother of a wealthy local rancher. For the duration of the film he has to find ways of defending his prisoner against the hired guns who are sent against him. In this he is assisted by Stumpy (Walter Brennan), a lame but feisty old man, Dude (Dean Martin), his former deputy who is attempting to recover from alcoholism caused by an unhappy love affair, and Colorado (Ricky Nelson), a youth who is quick with a gun but untested. As the film develops and the four companions are put under increasing pressure, we see them show their mettle. We also perceive the depth of affection which each has for the others.

Wayne had apparently been outraged by Fred Zinnemann's *High Noon* (1952), in which Sheriff Will Kane (Gary Cooper) throws down his star in disgust at the end of the film because he feels betrayed by the townspeople who have failed to help him. In *Rio Bravo*, the Wayne character relies not on ordinary people, non-professionals, but on a group of dedicated friends. 'A game-legged old man and a drunk? That's all you got?' Chance is asked. 'That's *what* I got,' he replies.

To complicate matters, the sheriff is drawn into a love affair with Feathers, a beautiful gambler (Angie Dickinson). Hawks brilliantly extracts the comedy inherent in Wayne's macho persona as the sheriff orders her out of town, only to find that she is running rings round him. In a masterly scene, the sheriff comes to her room to upbraid her. Instead, Feathers flirts with him so outrageously, in the process giving him instruction in how to kiss, that he is reduced to a stupefied silence, with Feathers putting into his mouth the words she wants him to say. At the end of the scene, Chance has no option but to offer a final, silent protest before exiting.

This love affair is equally matched by that between Chance and Dude, although this time Chance has the upper hand, forcing Dude to confront his demons, refusing to let him take the easy option of the bottle. In a memorable scene Chance appears to lose patience, telling Dude he doesn't care if he takes a drink. The result is that Dude, forced to take responsibility for himself, pours the whisky back into the bottle without spilling a drop.

Dimitri Tiomkin's score, based on Mexican folk tunes, is atmospheric and affords a charming interlude when Stumpy, Dude and Colorado sing a song, with Chance fondly looking on. A few years later, in 1966, Hawks directed *El Dorado*, a virtual remake, with Wayne playing a similar role, Robert Mitchum in the Dean Martin role, Arthur Hunnicutt playing the cranky old-timer and James Caan as the young man being initiated into the Hawksian pantheon of heroes.

Dir: Howard Hawks; **Prod**: Howard Hawks; **Scr**: Jules Furthman, Leigh Brackett; **DOP**: Russell Harlan; **Score**: Dimitri Tiomkin.

Rio Conchos
US, 1964 – 107 mins
Gordon Douglas

Gordon Douglas made Westerns for twenty-five years, some of them routine, others, such as his last one, *Barquero* (1970), agreeably full of quirky incident and off-beat characters. *Rio Conchos* is undoubtedly the best of the bunch. Stuart Whitman is Haven, an army officer who has mislaid a wagonload of repeating rifles. One of them turns up in the hands of Lassiter (Richard Boone), a former Confederate officer whose family have been murdered by Apaches and who has dedicated himself to revenge. Together with Sergeant Franklin (Jim Brown) and Rodriguez (Anthony Franciosa), a charming but untrustworthy Mexican, they journey south in search of the missing guns, driving a wagon full of gunpowder as a bargaining chip. Haven and Lassiter have taken an instant dislike to each other and their feuding continues all the way into Mexico. Fighting off some bandits, they are joined by a pretty Apache girl (Wende Wagner), in an improbably short skirt.

The first hour of the film is moderately entertaining. If Whitman is rather one-note, his face never departing from a scowl, Boone is as usual a personable antagonist, hard-drinking, cynical but given to expansive gestures. Having initially treated the black sergeant Franklin like a servant, he later beats a barman who will not serve Franklin because of his colour. Gradually Lassiter comes to believe in the mission and eventually is forced to kill Rodriguez when the latter wants to sell the gunpowder. However, Douglas saves the best part of the movie till last. The guns they seek have come into the possession of Theron Pardee (Edmund O'Brien). A demented Confederate veteran who had served as a guerrilla under Bedford Forrest, Pardee declares that the south lost the war because it was 'insufficiently ruthless'. He plans to fight the war again, without making the same mistake. The guns he has stolen from the US army he intends selling to the Apache, using the money to finance his private army.

Haven and Lassiter discover Pardee building a replica southern plantation mansion out in the desert. Captured and tortured by being dragged behind horses, they escape with the aid of the Apache girl, and the film has a spectacular finale as they explode their gunpowder under the guns, thus rendering them useless either to the Apaches or to Pardee's demented schemes. At the end, Pardee stands bemused as his half-built mansion burns down around him. O'Brien performs in his best scenery-chewing manner, this film sandwiched between his equally scene-stealing performances in *The Man Who Shot Liberty Valance* (1962) and *The Wild Bunch* (1969).

The film is determined to make its anti-racist points. The Apache leader Bloodshirt (Rodolfo Acosta) is as vicious as his name suggests, but the Apache girl aids Haven and Lassiter because she wants peace, and shows her sincerity by grieving for a dead white baby killed by her people. Though Jim Brown as Franklin has little to do but strangle a few Apaches, the initial antagonism in his relationship with Lassiter eventually turns to respect. American audiences might remember that Bedford Forrest was a founding member of the Ku Klux Klan.

Dir: Gordon Douglas; **Prod**: David Weisbart; **Scr**: Joseph Landon, Clair Huffaker; **DOP**: Joseph MacDonald; **Score**: Jerry Goldsmith.

Run of the Arrow
US, 1957 – 85 mins
Samuel Fuller

Sam Fuller's Sioux Indians are a singularly unconvincing bunch: Jay C. Flippen as the garrulous Walking Coyote, Spanish starlet Sarita Montiel as Yellow Moccasin, sexy in a tight deerskin dress slit up the thigh, and stony-faced Charles Bronson as Blue Buffalo, the chief. But ethnographic realism is not the point. Fuller is more interested in his highly schematic but daring analysis of nationalism and ethnic identity. O'Meara (Rod Steiger), a Confederate soldier of Irish extraction, fires the last bullet of the Civil War, wounding the Union officer Driscoll (Ralph Meeker). Disgusted with the Yankee invasion of the south and rejecting any

O'Meara (Rod Steiger, centre) in the camp of the Sioux in *Run of the Arrow*, with Blue Buffalo (Charles Bronson), Yellow Moccasin (Sarita Montiel) and Crazy Wolf (H. M. Wynant).

thought of reconciliation, O'Meara goes west. Captured by Indians, he is forced to undergo the 'run of the arrow' ordeal in which, given a start the length of one arrow shot, he is chased until he escapes or is killed. Yellow Moccasin saves him and O'Meara is adopted by her people, renouncing his origins. 'In my heart my nation is Sioux,' he says. A discussion of religion with Blue Buffalo results in a compromise: Americans and Sioux worship the same god, they just use a different name.

O'Meara's new allegiance is tested when Driscoll, recovered from his wound, comes west. One of his fellow officers, Captain Clark (Brian Keith) is a liberal, pointedly remarking that it's not Christian to hide under a white pillowcase and terrorise people. But Driscoll is a racist who is determined to beat the Indians by force. Put in charge of building a new fort, he provocatively locates it on Sioux hunting grounds. Steiger, who has been scouting for the army, now has to decide whether he can kill Americans if it comes to war. Yellow Moccasin has doubts: 'In my heart you were never a Sioux,' she says. 'You were born an American and what you are born you will die.' O'Meara tries to negotiate with Driscoll but is beaten. When the Sioux attack the fort Driscoll is captured and tortured. O'Meara once again loads the bullet he fired at the end of the war and shoots Driscoll dead in order to spare him further suffering. Thus, he can kill Americans, but only bad ones, and only to save them from the fate they deserve.

At the end Fuller deliberately leaves the question of O'Meara's allegiance open. Given a US flag by Yellow Moccasin, he rides off with the soldiers, but significantly he takes her with him, and also the Indian child they have adopted. On screen appear the words: 'The end of this story can only be written by you.' One implication is that racism is something which requires all of us to take a stand. But there is another: blood may be thicker than water, but nevertheless we can all choose our allegiances, at least to an extent.

Dir: Samuel Fuller; **Prod**: Samuel Fuller; **Scr**: Samuel Fuller; **DOP**: Joseph Biroc; **Score**: Victor Young.

The Searchers
US, 1956 – 119 mins
John Ford

A monumental film in every sense, and John Ford's masterpiece, the stature of *The Searchers* continues to grow. The story is simple enough. Returning from the Civil War, Ethan Edwards (John Wayne) is reunited with his brother Aaron and his wife Martha at their lonely ranch in Texas. Drawn away by a diversionary raid, Ethan returns to find Aaron and Martha murdered by the Comanche and their two daughters captured. Ethan and Martin Pawley (Jeffrey Hunter) give chase. Eventually one of the girls is discovered dead but the younger one, Debbie (Natalie Wood), cannot be found. Ethan and Martin refuse to give up and spend five long years tracking Debbie. At last they find her, the captive of a Comanche chief, Scar (Henry Brandon). At first reluctant to leave the Indians with whom she has become acculturated, Debbie is at last brought back safely.

What gives the film its compelling force is the character of Ethan, the most complex one that Wayne ever played. Ethan is an Indian-hater, a man who knows their ways but is implacably hostile. Debbie's capture makes him bitter and vindictive, almost to the point of madness, so that he prefers to see his niece dead rather than contemplate her as the sexual partner of Scar. His feelings are exacerbated by guilt at the memory that he himself loved his brother's wife; in raping Martha before murdering her, Scar has become a kind of monstrous surrogate for Ethan's own desires. At the end, Ethan confirms this identity by scalping the Comanche chief, a kind of symbolic castration asserting both Ethan's own savagery and his need to root out his quasi-incestuous desire. If, at the end Ethan appears to redeem himself, lifting his niece up in his arms as he says 'Let's go home, Debbie', in the final shot he is left outside in the wilderness, a man forever destined to be excluded from the warmth of the communal hearth.

Ford sets this narrative in Monument Valley (actually in Arizona, not Texas), one of seven Ford films to use this extraordinary location. The majesty of the great towers of red sandstone gives the story great resonance and grandeur, as the two searchers criss-cross the vast landscape in their dogged pursuit. But the narrative is also punctuated with comedy, much of it deriving from such minor characters as the Rev. Clayton (Ward Bond), frontier preacher and Texas Ranger, the crazed but visionary Mose (Hank Worden) and Charlie McCorry (Ken Curtis), the hick cowboy who is Martin's rival for the affections of Laurie (Vera Miles).

The 1950s was the heyday of the 'psychological' Western, with a series of tormented heroes. But none quite approaches the depth and complexity of Ethan, nor do any of the films quite match the magnificence of Ford's staging. In *The Searchers*, Ford's major themes such as the contrast of wilderness and garden and the centrality of home find their richest exploration.

Dir: John Ford; **Prod**: Merian C. Cooper; **Scr**: Frank S. Nugent; **DOP**: Winton C. Hoch; **Score**: Max Steiner.

Shane
US, 1953 – 118 mins
George Stevens

The artful framing of Shane as he rides down from the mountains, the man on horseback seen between the twin antlers of a deer, is perhaps just a touch too deliberate, evidence of a self-conscious attempt to make a classic. Yet classic the film undoubtedly is, on everyone's list of favourite Westerns and certainly a film of stature. Based on an excellent short novel by Jack Schaefer and with a screenplay by A. B. Guthrie Jr, author of *The Big Sky*, the film has a simple, elemental structure. Shane (Alan Ladd) rides in from nowhere and attaches himself to Joe Starrett (Van Heflin) and his family. Increasingly Shane is drawn into the feud between the small farmers of the valley and Ryker (Emil Meyer), a big rancher who covets their land. At one level it's a conflict between feudalism and the Jeffersonian ideal of yeoman farmers, seen as the bedrock of the democratic system. But the dispute is actually settled by the confrontation of Shane with Wilson, the hired gun brought in by Ryker to terrify the farmers. In a memorable scene, Wilson is first challenged by 'Stonewall' Torrey, a plucky but foolhardy southerner. Since Torrey is played by Elisha Cook Jr, Hollywood's eternal fall-guy, there can be only one outcome, with Torrey left prone in the mud as Wilson callously pleads self-defence.

The black-clad Wilson, played by Jack Palance as a sadistic killer, can only be beaten by a fellow professional. We learn nothing of Shane's previous history, but in an early scene he teaches Joe's hero-worshipping young son Joey (Brandon De Wilde) how to shoot, in the process demonstrating his own dazzling skill with a gun. Shane is a killer too, and once he has bested Wilson and settled the war on behalf of the farmers, he leaves the valley. As often with traditional Western heroes, though his violence is instrumental in making the frontier safe for decent people, the taint of death he carries with him cannot be accommodated in the newly domesticated west he leaves behind.

Starrett's wife Marion (Jean Arthur) objects to Shane tutoring her son in violence. She wishes for no guns in the valley, and at the end pleads with Shane not to go against Wilson. This too is traditional in the Western, dating at least as far back as Owen Wister's *The Virginian* (1902), in which Molly, the schoolteacher from the east, pleads with the hero not to go out and face the villain in the street. Barely a year before the release of *Shane* (1953), Grace Kelly had done the same in *High Noon* (1952), begging Gary Cooper to leave town rather than face up to the badmen.

The relationship between Marion and Shane is the most interesting in the film. From her first sighting of him, her gaze curious, voyeuristic as she stares at him from behind her curtains, it is clear she is drawn to him sexually, and Shane, buckskin-clad, blonde and blue-eyed, is a figure of desire. His ride away at the end is also a flight from the consequences of that attraction.

Dir: George Stevens; **Prod**: George Stevens; **Scr**: A. B. Guthrie Jr; **DOP**: Loyal Griggs; **Score**: Victor Young.

(*Opposite page*) Shane (Alan Ladd) shows hero-worshipping Joey (Brandon De Wilde) how to shoot in *Shane*

She Wore a Yellow Ribbon
US, 1949 – 103 mins
John Ford

'Feathered bonnets against the western sky,' intones the commentary, and John Ford never shot Indians more picturesquely than in this tale of army life in the south-west. The second of his so-called cavalry trilogy, after *Fort Apache*, is set in the period just after Custer's defeat in 1876, and plots its story of Indian warfare narrowly averted against the more intimate drama of the retirement of Captain Nathan Brittles (John Wayne). Brittles is given one last job before he leaves the army, escorting the Major's wife and niece to a stagecoach post so that they may safely leave the territory before Indians attack the fort. Brittles has to knock the heads together of two junior officers, Pennell (Harry Carey Jr) and Cohill (John Agar), who are feuding over the affections of the Major's niece Olivia (Joanne Dru). Before they reach their goal they come across a soldier wounded in an Indian attack, and when they reach the stage station they find it destroyed. Brittles leads the patrol back to the fort, leaving behind a small detachment to cover their retreat. Having delivered the women back to the fort, he wants to go out again, but is forbidden by the Major because his retirement date has arrived, and because the young officers must be allowed to take responsibility. The next morning Brittles apparently rides off to retirement in California. But he takes it upon himself to visit his old Indian friend Pony That Walks, trying to learn what he can about Indian plans, and then leads a force which drives away the Indian horses, thus averting their planned attack.

Supposedly this was Wayne's favourite of his performances, and it's certainly one of the most affecting, for example in the scenes when he communes with his dead wife at her graveside. Wayne's big scene is when he comes out in the morning of his retirement to find his whole troop lined up waiting for him, and he's presented with a watch. He makes a business of getting out his spectacles to read the 'sentiments' on the back, as a way of disguising his tears. Ford's first colour film to be set in his beloved Monument Valley, it's beautifully shot, not least in the scene when the wounded soldier is carried in a wagon through the middle of Monument Valley in a thunderstorm. For his work on the film, cameraman Winton Hoch won an Oscar.

A familiar Fordian motif is the essential unity of the United States, strained but not ruptured by the Civil War, and when a soldier of southern origins dies at the stage station Sergeant Tyree (Ben Johnson) asks permission for a Confederate flag to be placed on his coffin. The film has plenty of Ford's trademark broad comedy, with Victor McLaglen as the hard-drinking Quincannon, and the successful conclusion of Brittles' mission is marked in typical Fordian style with a dance.

Dir: John Ford; **Prod**: John Ford, Merian C. Cooper; **Scr**: Frank S. Nugent, Lawrence Stallings; **DOP**: Winton C. Hoch; **Score**: Richard Hageman.

The Shooting
US, 1966 – 81 mins
Monte Hellman

The legendary producer of low-budget genre films, Roger Corman, gave director Monte Hellman and star Jack Nicholson (who also produced) the total of $150,000 to shoot two Westerns back to back. The result was *The Shooting* and its companion piece, *Ride in the Whirlwind* (1965). In the former, Warren Oates plays Gashade, a bounty hunter now turned miner, who gets back to his claim to find his terrified partner Coley (Will Hutchins) in hiding after an unknown gunman has shot another miner, Leland Drum (B. J. Merholz). It appears that Drum and Gashade's brother had accidentally killed someone in the nearby town and Gashade's brother has run off. A shot is heard and we see a hand pointing a gun at a horse's head, then a woman (Millie Perkins) appears out of the wilderness. She never identifies herself, but persuades a reluctant Gashade to guide her to the town of Kingsley in exchange for $1,000. The childlike Coley accompanies them and soon falls for the Woman, but Gashade is indifferent ('Pretty ain't nothing'). Gashade suspects someone is following, and before long Billy Spear (Jack Nicholson) rides into their camp. Dressed in a white shirt, with a black waistcoat and gloves, Spear is clearly a professional gunfighter, and it emerges that it is he who shot Leland Drum. The four head off into the desert, apparently in pursuit of someone, though the Woman will not say who. Eventually Spear shoots Coley, and Gashade buries him. Gashade and Spear fight and Gashade smashes Spear's shooting hand to prevent another killing, but the Woman chases their quarry into the rocks and shoots him; it is Gashade's twin brother.

Hellman's next film after this was *Two-Lane Blacktop* (1971), a road movie that became a cult film, and *The Shooting* is also a road movie of sorts, taking place almost entirely along a dusty trail through the desert. It's a film in which the characters have been reduced to the bare essentials, stripped of community and social context. As Gashade, Oates maintains a glum, slightly puzzled stoicism, while Nicholson is saturnine, conveying plenty of menace but little of the charm that was to emerge in his later roles. Perkins plays the Woman as petulant and bossy, forever making impossible demands while flirting with the childish Coley.

Hellman's direction, with extreme close-ups and a frequently disorienting spatial organisation of the scene, does not make for comfortable viewing, nor is he overly concerned with the niceties of the traditional Western; at one point Coley even mounts his horse from the right. Predictably, the film did not achieve financial success. But though

Sinister gunfighter Billy Spear (Jack Nicholson) with 'the Woman' (Millie Perkins) in the minimalist *The Shooting*

the ending is at once corny and predictable, both the elemental quality of the struggle against nature (the desert is pitiless, wearing down both horses and humans) and the battle of wills between the characters makes for an unusual experience, perhaps the nearest to an avant-garde Western that American cinema approached until Jim Jarmusch's *Dead Man* (1995).

Dir: Monte Hellman; **Prod**: Jack Nicholson, Monte Hellman; **Scr**: Adrien Joyce; **DOP**: Gregory Sandor; **Score**: Richard Markowitz.

The Shootist
US, 1976 – 100 mins
Don Siegel

Based on an excellent novel by Glendon Swarthout, this is the story of an ageing gunfighter's last days. It is 1901; Queen Victoria has just died and Carson City is rapidly modernising, with streetcars and electricity. J. B Books (John Wayne) is a throwback to the earlier, wilder days of the old west: 'To put it in a nutshell,' he is told, 'you've outlived your time.' He pays a visit to the elderly Dr Hofstetler (James Stewart) who confirms his fears that he has terminal bowel cancer. Books decides to stay on and await death in Carson City, and Hofstetler recommends lodging with Mrs Rogers (Lauren Bacall), a widow with an adolescent son, Gillom (Ron Howard). Knowing his fame will attract attention, Books tries to remain anonymous but thanks to the garrulous local marshal (Harry Morgan) his secret is soon out. Mrs Rogers is at first fearful of Books, then outraged when a gunfight breaks out in the night as two men try to gain a reputation by killing him. The other guests leave. But gradually Books and his landlady develop a mutual affection. Gillom hero-worships him and persuades Books to give him a shooting lesson. When Hofstetler suggests that suicide might be preferable to an agonising death, Books conceives a plan. After careful preparation, including having his suit cleaned by the new dry-cleaning process, Books goes down to the saloon on his birthday, having arranged to meet three men. One is the local gambler Pulford (Hugh O'Brian), another is an old enemy, Sweeney (Richard Boone), while the third, Cobb (Bill McKinney), is a local bully who has offended Books. All these men are eager to take on a man whom they believe is too ill to defend himself. In a violent shootout Books gets the better of all three, but is himself shot in the back by the bartender. Gillom picks up Books's gun and shoots the bartender, then throws it away.

John Wayne was himself suffering from cancer at the time he made this film, his last. It is both a brave and an exceptionally skilled performance, avoiding the slightest hint of the mawkishness that would seem to be inherent in the subject. The film begins with a tongue-in-cheek biography of Books which is in fact a montage of scenes from Wayne's earlier films, and it is clear that the film has an additional level of resonance not present in the original novel, being a celebration of Wayne himself as much as an elegy to the old west. But Wayne, while expansive, even larger than life, never descends into self-parody.

Lauren Bacall offers solid support as the starchy landlady who gradually unbends as Books reveals his need for her, despite Books's rejection of her attempts to push religion on him ('My church has been the mountains and solitude'). Elsewhere the film offers a series of meaty cameos to familiar faces who, besides those already listed, include John Carradine as an undertaker with an eye on the main chance, and Scatman Crothers as the wily manager of a livery stable.

Dir: Don Siegel; Prod: M. J. Frankovich, William Self; Scr: Miles Hood Swarthout, Scott Hale; DOP: Bruce Surtees; Score: Elmer Bernstein.

Stagecoach
US, 1939 – 97 mins
John Ford

The 1930s wasn't a great decade for the Western. After a few expensive flops such as *The Big Trail* (1930) and *Cimarron* (1930) the major studios largely abandoned the genre to Poverty Row producers making cheap B-features. John Ford hadn't made a Western for a dozen years when he cast John Wayne and Claire Trevor in a story about a stagecoach ride through dangerous Indian territory. In trying to sell it to producer David O. Selznick, Ford described *Stagecoach* as a 'classic Western', a cut above the B-Westerns which Wayne himself had been making. One thing this meant was giving it more appeal to women in the audience. So Ford and screenwriter Dudley Nichols added to the original tale by Ernest Haycox a more developed love story and the birth of a baby en route. But this was not enough for Selznick, who looked down his nose and passed on the project.

. Not that the film stints on the more traditional satisfactions of the genre. The last part of the film packs in plenty of action, including a gunfight between Wayne and the Plummer gang and a stirring Indian attack as the stagecoach careers across the flat desert. The sequence was enriched by some superlative stuntwork by Yakima Canutt, who, playing one of the Apache attackers, leaps on to one of the stage's horses, is then shot and has to fall between the horses' hooves and under the wheels.

This was John Wayne's second chance at major stardom after the failure of *The Big Trail*, and he took it with both hands. From his first entrance, standing in the desert waving down the stage, he cuts an impressive figure as the Ringo Kid, who has busted out of jail in order to be revenged on the Plummers, who have killed his father and brother. But Wayne's appearance is delayed while Ford explores the characters of the other travellers on the coach. Each is deftly and memorably sketched in: Dallas (Claire Trevor), the girl who is no better than she should be and who is run out of town together with drunken Doc Boone (Thomas Mitchell) by the puritanical ladies of the Law and Order League; Peacock (Donald Meek), a timorous whisky salesman; Hatfield (John Carradine), a southern gambler; Mrs Mallory (Louise Platt), the pregnant wife of a cavalry officer; and Gatewood (Berton Churchill), a banker who is making off with the assets. On the outside of the coach are Buck (Andy Devine), the portly driver, and Curly (George Bancroft), the local sheriff. The interaction between this oddly assorted group allows Ford to

John Ford's first use of the majestic location of Monument Valley, in *Stagecoach*

explore a cherished theme, the superior moral qualities of those whom 'respectable' society disdains.

This was the first film Ford shot in Monument Valley, a landscape of towering sandstone buttes on the border between Utah and Arizona. As the tiny stagecoach makes its way through the vastness of the desert, the frailty of its occupants is doubly emphasised as the camera tracks towards a group of Indians observing its progress. Ford makes no attempt to present the Indians as individuals; they are merely a force of nature.

The film's healthy performance at the box office helped re-establish the Western genre.

Dir: John Ford; **Prod**: Walter Wanger; **Scr**: Dudley Nichols; **DOP**: Bert Glennon; **Score**: Richard Hageman, Franke Harling, John Leipold, Leo Shuken, Louis Gruenberg.

Support Your Local Sheriff!
US, 1969 – 92 mins
Burt Kennedy

In most Western comedies, the humour is at the expense of the
unquestioned masculinity and courage which are perceived to be at the
heart of the genre. In the case of *Support Your Local Sheriff!* it's not so
much that Jason McCullough (James Garner) is a coward, rather that his
methods of operation are unconventional and often downright devious.
Essentially the film is a satire on the town-tamer subgenre, with specific
references to such classics as *My Darling Clementine* (1946), *Rio Bravo*
(1959) and *High Noon* (1952). Following a gold strike (in a freshly dug
grave) in a nondescript Western town, chaos ensues. The mayor (Harry
Morgan) and town council resolve to hire a sheriff, and McCullough
volunteers, though declaring that he is only passing through on his way
to Australia. McCullough is accommodated at the house of the mayor,
whose eccentric daughter Prudy (Joan Hackett) cooks dinner, managing
to set light to herself in the process. When interviewed for the job,
McCullough repeats the trick performed by James Stewart in *Winchester
'73* (1950), shooting a hole through a washer tossed in the air. Now he
sets about cleaning up the town, shooting a few obstreperous cowboys.
In this task he enlists the help of the town drunk Jake (Jack Elam), who is
reluctantly enrolled as deputy. McCullough succeeds in arresting Joe
Danby (Bruce Dern), the dim-witted son of old man Danby (Walter
Brennan), who bullies the local townspeople. Brennan, reprising his role
as Old Man Clanton in *My Darling Clementine*, comes into town to
demand that Joe be released. In an inspired piece of comic business, he
draws his gun and pokes it menacingly at McCullough, who pushes his
finger up the barrel. Nonplussed, Danby allows himself to be disarmed.

Danby decides to marshal all his forces. The town council holds a
meeting and, just as in *High Noon*, the citizens fall over each other in
their eagerness to find reasons why they should not assist their sheriff,
much to the disgust of Prudy, who has fallen for the sheriff, even though

she won't admit it. When the Danby gang ride into town they find Joe bound over the barrel of a cannon pointing up Main Street. This is sufficient to secure their disarmament. McCullough agrees to marry Prudy while still muttering about Australia, and Jake delivers a direct-to-camera coda on how McCullough became governor of the state and how he, Jake, became 'one of the most beloved characters in Western folklore'.

The film was highly successful and two years later a sequel appeared, *Support Your Local Gunfighter*, with several of the same cast, including Garner and Elam. Though he is ably supported by the cast of Western veterans, it's Garner who is largely responsible for the film's easy-going but witty style. His performance honed by his role as the cynical but engaging Maverick in the long-running TV series, Garner's comic style seems effortless, registering with a perfectly deadpan expression the information that Prudy is an heiress and that anyone who marries her gets a goldmine, 'shaft and all'.

Dir: Burt Kennedy; **Prod**: William Bowers; **Scr**: William Bowers, **DOP**: Harry Stradling Jr; **Score**: Jeff Alexander.

The Tall Men
US, 1955 – 121 mins
Raoul Walsh

Montana 1866. Texan Ben Allison (Clark Gable) has come north with his
brother Clint (Cameron Mitchell), anxious to leave behind unpleasant
memories of the Civil War. Riding through the Rockies they see a man
hanging from a tree. 'Looks like we're getting close to civilisation,' Ben
remarks ironically. Down on their luck, they arrive in a small mining town
and rob the wealthy Nathan Stark (Robert Ryan), taking him with them
on the trail to prevent him sounding the alarm. Forceful and persuasive,
Stark persuades them that they could do better for themselves if they
threw in their lot with his plan to drive cattle up from Texas to the
Montana goldfields. Though sceptical they agree to ride south with Stark
through heavy snow. On the way they encounter Nella Turner (Jane
Russell), who is marooned and starving. Stark wants to press on. But Ben
goes back to rescue Nella from Indian attack. In a lengthy scene of
initially good-natured banter, their relationship blossoms, but Nella has
big dreams, while Ben just wants to settle down in a Texas backwater.
They fall out, and when they get to San Antonio, Nella allows Stark to
court her with expensive dresses and champagne.

The three men assemble a huge herd of cattle and prepare to drive
them north. Stark insists on bringing Nella along. As is traditional in
cattle-driving Westerns, they have to negotiate natural obstacles such as
rivers, and meet the threat of bushwhackers and hostile Indians. Clint's
drinking becomes a problem and in order to protect him from Stark's
increasing animosity Ben sends him to ride point; later Ben finds his
brother shot full of arrows. Having driven the herd clean through the
marauding bands of Red Cloud's Sioux, Ben and Stark reach journey's
end. When Ben goes to be paid off, Stark tries to arrest him for his
earlier act of robbery with the aid of the town vigilante group, but Ben
has brought his Mexican *vaqueros* along and takes the money due him.
Returning to his camp, he finds Nella waiting for him.

This is a handsome movie, impressively shot in CinemaScope in the snowy wastes of the mountains and the cactus-strewn deserts of the south-west. Russell gets to play a lot of her scenes in fancy underwear, and she and Gable work up a good head of steam with their verbal jousting; at one point he has to cut her out of an over-tight corset, because, he says, she is breathing 'like an old swamp frog'. But the film also has a theme of sorts. Stark is the prototype northern capitalist, always figuring out the money angles (cattle can be bought for three or four dollars a head in Texas and sold for fifty in Montana). Nella thinks she wants his kind of success, yet knows that he views people much as he does cattle ('I don't like being weighed, measured and counted,' she remarks when he looks her up and down). As so often in the Western, southern charm and warmth eventually win out over northern calculation.

Dir: Raoul Walsh; **Prod**: William A. Bacher, William Hawks; **Scr**: Sydney Boehm, Frank S. Nugent; **DOP**: Leo Tover; **Score**: Victor Young.

The Tall T
US, 1956 – 77 mins
Budd Boetticher

The first of five Westerns that Budd Boetticher made with producer Harry
Joe Brown, all starring Randolph Scott, *The Tall T* has, like several of
Boetticher's Westerns, a script by Burt Kennedy, later to become a
successful director of Westerns in his own right. Typically, the dialogue is

Pat Brennan (Randolph Scott) gets the drop on Frank (Richard Boone) in *The Tall T*, while
Doretta (Maureen O'Sullivan) seeks protection

laced with spare but pithy remarks expressive both of character and of an ethos in which no words are wasted. However, investigation shows that much of the dialogue is lifted almost intact from the pages of the original short story by Elmore Leonard on which the film is based. When first published the title was 'The Captives'; there does not seem to be an adequate explanation of why the title was changed or what exactly 'the tall T' is, though it may refer to the Tenvoorde ranch which the hero visits at the start of the film.

Scott plays Pat Brennan, a top ramrod who is now trying to be an independent rancher. Losing his horse in a wager, he has to walk home until he is picked up by a stagecoach driven by his friend Rintoon (Arthur Hunnicutt). The coach contains Willard Mims (John Hubbard) and his new wife Doretta (Maureen O'Sullivan), a wealthy heiress. At the next stage station they are held up by three men: Frank (Richard Boone), Chink (Henry Silva) and Billy Jack (Skip Homeier). Rintoon is shot and Brennan learns that the station manager and his young son have been murdered and thrown down the well. Willard is a coward who suggests that the gang ransom his wife, as a way of saving his own skin. While they wait for the ransom to be negotiated, Brennan engages in a battle of wits with the gang in order to secure his own survival and that of Doretta. Brennan manages to isolate the three men from each other and eventually picks them off one at a time.

The artistry of the film comes in the interplay between Brennan and the three outlaws, and in his developing relationship with the woman. She discovers that her husband has betrayed her, and then sees him murdered, but Brennan brings her out of despair and, by refusing to indulge her self-pity, enables her to play a vital role in their deliverance.

Frank is another of Boetticher's personable villains. Despising his two companions ('Nothing but animals'), he is keen to talk to Brennan as a man he can respect about his desire to settle down ('A man should have something of his own, something to belong to'). But for those he despises, like the craven Willard Mims, he shows no mercy, deceiving him into thinking he may go free, then chillingly ordering his destruction:

'Bust him, Chink.' Scott is wonderful as the stoical Brennan, making each word count, waiting his moment. He provides a typically terse yet eloquent explanation to Doretta of why Western heroes act as they do: 'There's some things a man can't ride around.' The film is shot almost entirely on location, near Lone Pine in California, where Boetticher finds great beauty in the harsh desert landscape.

Dir: Budd Boetticher; **Prod**: Harry Joe Brown; **Scr**: Burt Kennedy; **DOP**: Charles Lawton Jr; **Score**: Heinz Roemheld.

Tears of the Black Tiger/Fa Talai Jone
Thailand, 2001 – 101 mins
Wisit Sasanatieng

Eastern Westerns are not the rarities they might seem. The great
Japanese director Akira Kurosawa learned from John Ford, and
Hollywood repaid the compliment by re-making his masterpiece *The
Seven Samurai* as *The Magnificent Seven* (1960), while Sergio Leone
borrowed from Kurosawa's *Yojimbo* (1961) when he directed *A Fistful of
Dollars* (1964). More recently Jackie Chan had great success with
Shanghai Noon (2000), grafting martial arts onto the Western. *Tears of
the Black Tiger* may be fundamentally a love story in which poor boy
Dum (Chartchai Ngamsan) and rich girl Rumpoey (Stella Malucchi) defy
parental disapproval and rampaging bandits, but it makes liberal use of
the iconography of the Western. The costumes of the bandits and the
props draw heavily on singing cowboy films of the 1930s and 40s, with
hand-tooled boots and gaudily embroidered shirts which Gene Autry
would have been proud of. Dum shows evidence of sartorial
independence by wearing his gun in a shoulder holster, but his habit of
spitting seems a straight copy from Clint Eastwood in *The Outlaw Josey
Wales* (1976). Director Wisit Sasanatieng shoots his gunfights in the style
of Eastwood's mentor Leone, with extreme close-ups of eyes and
gunbelts, even copying the moment in *Once Upon a Time in the West*
(1968) when the water drips onto Woody Strode's hat. The bandits ride
out to the sound of Ennio Morricone-style whistling on the soundtrack,
while a close-up of two bullets meeting in mid-air could have come
straight from Sam Raimi's *The Quick and the Dead* (1995), a film clearly
influenced by spaghetti Westerns.

The film begins some time in the 1940s, when Dum and Rumpoey
meet in the Thai countryside. They row out in a boat to a beautiful
pagoda. On the way back they are attacked by thugs. Dum fights them
off and Rumpoey gives him a silver harmonica as a keepsake. Later they
meet as students in the city. Once more Dum rescues her from danger

and she agrees to marry him. Back in the countryside Dum's father is murdered by a local bandit and, in order to avenge him, Dum joins a gang of bandits, his exploits earning him the name of the 'Black Tiger'. Rumpoey's father insists that she marry Kumjorn (Arawat Ruangvuth), a police captain. When Kumjorn is captured by the bandits, Dum sets him free. Reluctantly Rumpoey agrees to wed Kumjorn, but Dum, still in love with her, warns her father that the bandits plan to attack on the day of the wedding. His warning is ignored and the bandits carry off Rumpoey. Once more Dum rescues her, but this time he is shot.

The chief pleasure of the film is in its stunning visuals, with the screen saturated in hues of turquoise, pink and lime-green. This is reminiscent not so much of B-Westerns themselves, which were mostly in black and white, as of the stencil-coloured stills displayed outside the movie houses where they were shown. This effect was obtained by transferring the film negative to video and digitally altering it before putting it back on celluloid, with a result that makes for a strikingly post-modern Western.

Dir: Wisit Sasanatieng; **Prod**: Nonzee Nimibutr; **Scr**: Wisit Sasanatieng; **DOP**: Nattawut Kittikhun; **Score**: Amornpong Methakunawut.

Terror in a Texas Town
US, 1958 – 81 mins
Joseph H. Lewis

This is the last movie Western directed by the legendary Joseph H. Lewis, specialist in B-feature Westerns and films noirs. It has all of Lewis's characteristically doom-laden melodrama and almost surreal bizarreness. In Prairie City, the epicurean McNeil (Sebastian Cabot) dines on lobster and champagne while he plots to take over the land of the local small farmers, who are too craven to stand up against him. Unknown to them McNeil has discovered that oil is present. His enforcer is Johnny Crale (Ned Young), a black-clad gunfighter who wears gloves in order to hide the fact that his right hand has been shot away and replaced by a steel claw. Johnny guns down Hansen, an elderly Swedish farmer, whose seaman son, George (Sterling Hayden), arrives to inherit the property. Wearing the kind of hat that denotes a hick, with a suit two sizes too small and a heavy Swedish accent, George obstinately refuses to be frightened off. Exasperated, McNeil remarks that 'Swedes in this country, they keep popping up like jack-rabbits.' Johnny's girlfriend Molly (Carol Kelly), a sad-faced brassy blonde straight out of film noir, knows the gunfighter is doomed ('One man with a gun just can't make it any more') but can't summon up the courage to leave him. As she explains to George, who else would have her? Beaten up by McNeil's men, George is thrown onto a train, but stubbornly walks back to town, where he finds that his friend, Mexican farmer José (Victor Millan), has been murdered by Johnny. Seizing his father's harpoon, George marches into town. By this time Johnny has turned against the arrogant McNeil and killed him. The townspeople form up behind George as Johnny comes out onto the street to confront him. Taunting the Swede, Johnny goes for his gun but is skewered before he can get off a shot.

   Shot in stark black and white, this conflict between homespun virtue and evil incarnate has the courage of its convictions. Johnny is a compelling villain, bursting into his room after a confrontation with

George (Sterling Hayden) shows his friend José (Victor Millan) the harpoon which belonged to his father and which will feature in the last scene of *Terror in a Texas Town*

McNeil, who has called him a cripple, and berating his girlfriend for still being in bed, then when she gets up to remonstrate with him snapping at her to get back in bed where she belongs. There's a clear implication that Johnny is not only missing a hand but is impotent too. By the end he has become traumatised by his murder of the Mexican, who had refused to kneel before being shot. Repeating over and over to anyone who will listen, Johnny says he has at last met a man who doesn't fear death, and the experience has unnerved him to the point where his final ritual meeting in the street with the harpoon-wielding George amounts almost to suicide. Though credited to Ben Perry, the script was written by Dalton Trumbo while he was blacklisted.

Dir: Joseph H. Lewis; **Prod**: Frank Seltzer; **Scr**: Ben L. Perry; **DOP**: Ray Rennahan; **Score**: Gerald Fried.

3.10 to Yuma
US, 1957 – 92 mins
Delmer Daves

Based on a story by Elmore Leonard, this is a tight and tense drama in the manner of *High Noon* (1952). Dan Evans (Van Heflin) is a small rancher whose cattle are dying in the drought but who cannot afford to buy water. Ben Wade (Glenn Ford) and his gang hold up the local stage and Wade kills the driver. Wade lingers in Bisbee in order to dally with saloon girl Emmy (Felicia Farr) and is captured. Afraid Wade's gang will return to rescue him, stage owner Butterfield (Robert Emhardt) offers Dan two hundred dollars to escort Wade to Contention, where he can be put on the 3.10 train to Yuma. The only man willing to assist Dan is the town drunk Potter (Henry Jones). Reaching Contention in the early morning, Dan has several hours to guard his prisoner in the hotel before the train arrives. The brother of the shot stagecoach driver bursts in and tries to murder Wade but Dan saves him. When Wade's gang arrives in town, the assistance that Butterfield has recruited fades away, rather as in *High Noon* the townspeople desert Marshal Will Kane in his hour of need. Potter is murdered by the gang and Dan is left alone to walk Wade to the train, with the gang lying in wait.

Heflin and Ford are a perfect contrast as Dan and Wade, the former honest, sincere and dull, Wade ruthless but charming and self-confident. Wade announces his callousness in his cold-blooded shooting of the stage driver, but he has no trouble in seducing the pretty saloon girl. During their long wait together in the hotel room, he knows exactly how to get under Dan's skin, playing on his fears of financial ruin, probing at the security of Dan's marriage. Earlier, on the way to Contention, Dan and Potter had stopped off at Dan's ranch with their prisoner, and Wade had a chance to observe Dan's wife. Now, as the moment of truth gets closer, Wade taunts Dan with his inability to buy nice things for his wife: 'I bet she was a real beautiful girl before she met you.'

George Duning's theme song is sung over the opening credits by Frankie Laine, and whistled by Ben Wade as he lies at ease on the hotel bed, confident of being set free by his friends. The last half hour of the film plays out almost in real time as the clock moves round to three. The tension is wound tighter and tighter as Dan's allies desert him ('We've got families,' they plead). At the end even Butterfield is begging Dan to let Wade go, offering to pay him the $200 anyway. But by now it's pride not money that motivates Dan, and at the last moment Wade reveals his admiration for Dan's courage, agreeing to leap on the train. As the train pulls out of the station, with Dan waving to his wife, it begins to rain.

Dir: Delmer Daves; **Prod**: David Heilweil; **Scr**: Halsted Welles; **DOP**: Charles Lawton Jr; **Score**: George Duning.

Two Rode Together
US, 1961 – 109 mins
John Ford

John Ford didn't like this film much, telling Peter Bogdanovich that he only made it as a favour to Harry Cohn, head of Columbia Pictures. But it makes a fascinating companion piece to *The Searchers* (1956). It's another captivity narrative, but from a different perspective. Instead of a deeply troubled Indian-fighter trying to rescue the daughter of his beloved sister-in-law, the hero is the cynical and venal sheriff of Tascosa, a sleepy south-western town. Guthrie McCabe (James Stewart) is dragooned by his old friend Lt Jim Gary (Richard Widmark) into redeeming white captives from the Comanche. At the army fort the commander (John McIntire) is disgusted by McCabe's mercenary attitude but reluctantly concedes McCabe's demand that he get from the captives' relatives any money that he can.

Before setting off McCabe meets the relatives, among them Knudsen (John Qualen), who still wants his little girl back even though McCabe paints an ugly picture of her life as a Comanche's wife. Marty (Shirley Jones) is a young woman who blames herself for her brother's capture, while Wringle (Willis Bouchey) will accept any captive for his grieving wife just as long as he can get back to his business. In the Comanche camp McCabe and Gary negotiate with chief Quanah Parker (Henry Brandon). An elderly white woman, Hanna Clegg (Mae Marsh) refuses to go back with them, fearing the consequences, but in exchange for rifles, they buy the freedom of a young boy, Running Wolf (David Kent), despite his having lost all traces of his white upbringing. And they also come away with a Mexican captive, Elena (Linda Cristal), the wife of Quanah Parker's rival Stone Calf (Woody Strode). Back at the fort, Running Wolf escapes, murders a white woman and is lynched. At a dance, during which Gary proposes to Marty, Elena is severely embarrassed by the prurience and racism of the soldiers' wives, and declares she wishes she had stayed with the Comanche. McCabe defends her stoutly, and again later when she is insulted by the madame of the whorehouse in Tascosa. He and Elena leave on a stagecoach for California.

In *The Searchers* Debbie is welcomed back into the community with open arms. In *Two Rode Together*, when the captives return to white society their troubles are just beginning. McCabe's apparent cynicism is ultimately vindicated as no more than a clear-sighted view of the realities of reintegration. His acceptance of Elena, despite her sexual experiences with the Comanche, is in stark contrast to Ethan Edwards's obsession with Debbie's 'contamination'.

Not that the film is an arid demonstration of racism. The first fifteen minutes especially are a delight, with Stewart and Widmark playing off each other in some wonderful comedy. At one point the two sit side by side on a river bank, in a single take that lasts a full four minutes, and discourse upon their contrasting lives. Gary is amazed to discover that McCabe gets ten per cent of everything in Tascosa, including the whorehouse takings. McCabe's defence is unabashed: 'You're a man of modest wants, I just require a little more.'

Dir: John Ford; **Prod**: Stan Shpetner; **Scr**: Frank S. Nugent; **DOP**: Charles Lawton Jr; **Score**: George Duning.

Ulzana's Raid
US, 1972 – 103 mins
Robert Aldrich

Loosely based on an episode in 1885 when a Chiricahua Apache, Ulzana, broke out of the reservation with a dozen companions, Aldrich's film appears to position itself in opposition to the liberal films about Indians of the 1950s, as well as contemporary pro-Indian films such as *Little Big Man* (1970). Whereas the earlier films had shown the Indians as more sinned against than sinning, and insisted that they were at heart just normal human beings like the rest of us, *Ulzana's Raid* insists upon the radical Otherness of the Indian. The Apaches torture and mutilate white men. At one point they cut out the heart of a young soldier and toss it playfully among themselves. A white woman is raped nearly to death. So graphic is the violence that some shots were cut from the original British release.

The soldiers are mostly raw recruits, initially seen playing baseball, a clear indication of their boyish lack of military experience. The young army lieutenant (Bruce Davison) leading the pursuit of Ulzana is the son of a minister of religion and of the opinion that the root of the Indian problem is a lack of Christian feeling towards the Apache. He cross-questions his Apache scout, Ke-Ni-Tay (Jorge Luke), seeking to understand their behaviour.

'Why are your people like that? Why are they so cruel?

'Is how they are.'

'But why?'

'Is how they are, they have always been that way.'

Easy answers are not what the film is interested in providing. However, it is less about trying to understand Indians than it is about white attitudes to them. Whites too are not above vindictive violence, as revealed when some soldiers mutilate the body of a dead Apache. The young lieutenant is appalled by this action. The grizzled veteran scout MacIntosh (an excellent performance by Burt Lancaster) observes his naivety. Despite having an Indian wife, MacIntosh has no illusions about Indians; though he doesn't hate them he is scared of them. As he sardonically remarks, the soldiers' behaviour 'kind of confuses the issue, don't it?'

At times almost sadistic in its desire to rub our noses in the Apaches' cruelty, the film is ultimately bracing in its refusal to sentimentalise. Aldrich expertly keeps the action moving against the harsh greys and yellows of the desert landscape, extracting pleasure from the manoeuvres and counter-manoeuvres of pursuers and pursued, each trying to guess the other's next move. In the course of the action Ulzana's young son, who accompanies him on the raid, is killed, but Aldrich and his screenwriter Alan Sharp resist the opportunity to milk easy tears. Ulzana himself scarcely appears on screen; a shadowy, elusive figure, he is the stuff of nightmares. At last he is tracked down and killed by Ke-Ni-Tay, but not before MacIntosh has received a fatal wound. Spurning assistance the scout chooses to die a stoic's death, defiantly defending himself against the remnants of Ulzana's band.

Dir: Robert Aldrich; **Prod**: Carter De Haven; **Scr**: Alan Sharp; **DOP**: Joseph Biroc; **Score**: Frank De Vol.

Unforgiven
US, 1992 – 131 mins
Clint Eastwood

Hailed almost unanimously by critics as a 'revisionist' Western, Clint
Eastwood's most recent excursion out west cunningly attempts to have
its cake and eat it too. On the one hand, it tries to distance itself from
the celebration of violence which the traditional Western has been
accused of. William Munny (Clint Eastwood) is an ageing, unsuccessful
pig farmer trying to bring up two children after the death of his wife,
who made him renounce his previous career as a cold-eyed killer. He is
tempted into one last job by the Schofield Kid (Jaimz Woolvett) , a brash
young man who fancies himself as a gunman. Up in Wyoming a group
of prostitutes is offering a reward for revenge against a cowboy who has
knifed one of them. In a genre not noted for its pro-female attitudes,
Munny's mission seems designed to strike a blow for feminism and at
the same time show the evil effects of violence.

However, things do not work out as planned, for Munny and the
Kid, accompanied by Will's old friend Ned (Morgan Freeman), have not
reckoned with Sheriff Little Bill Daggett (Gene Hackman), who has
already run one aspiring claimant of the reward out of town. Munny and
the Kid eventually manage to kill the offending cowboy but Ned is
beaten to death by Little Bill. At this moment, motivated by rage at the
loss of his friend, Munny casts aside his wife's teaching against violence
and the film delivers all the traditional satisfactions of the genre as he
wreaks a terrible revenge on Little Bill and his henchmen.

It's a film filled with consummate performances. Richard Harris is
superb as English Bob, the dandified bounty hunter humiliated by Little
Bill. And Hackman is chilling as Little Bill himself, dispensing self-
righteous homilies as he practises his hopeless carpentry skills or
sadistically beats up those who dare to challenge him. Hackman won an
Oscar, as did Eastwood himself, but for direction, not acting, even
though it's undoubtedly one of his best performances, digging deep into

the character of a man who is torn between his reformed present and a terrible past.

David Webb Peoples' script had passed through several hands in Hollywood before Eastwood committed to it. The dialogue deliberately tries for a stilted, Victorian feel, the characters all in some sense playing roles, liking the sound of their own voices. This is a point underlined by the presence of W. W. Beauchamp (Saul Rubinek), a hack writer of dime novels who assiduously notes down English Bob's vainglorious observations before opportunistically transferring his allegiance to Little Bill. Physically it's a very dark film to look at, with its shadowy interiors full of chiaroscuro and bleak, wintry landscapes. Every effort has been taken to give the film an authentic period feel, but ultimately it's a drama of elemental, archetypal emotions, a distillation of the genre's perennial appeal, setting a good man, however flawed, against the bad. Eastwood dedicated the film to Don Siegel and Sergio Leone, his two mentors from his early days.

Dir: Clint Eastwood; **Prod**: Clint Eastwood; **Scr**: David Webb Peoples; **DOP**: Jack N. Green; **Score**: Lennie Niehaus.

The Unforgiven
US, 1959 – 125 mins
John Huston

Based on a novel by Alan LeMay, who also wrote the source novel for *The Searchers* (1956), this offers a captivity narrative in reverse. Kelsey (Joseph Wiseman), a crazed old man with a sabre, announces to Rachel Zachary (Audrey Hepburn) that he is 'the sword of God . . . whereby the wrong shall be righted and the truth shall be told'. Rachel's mother (Lillian Gish) clearly knows something but is not saying. Rachel has three brothers: Andy (Doug McClure), too young to have tasted beer yet, Cash (Audie Murphy), who is a racist ('If the wind's in the right direction I can smell Indian a mile off') and Ben (Burt Lancaster), the rock that they all depend on. Charlie (Albert Salmi), the son of their neighbour, wants to marry Rachel. Then Kiowa Indians appear outside their lonely sod house on the prairie. The Indians say that Rachel is one of their own, and one of them claims to be her brother. Ben sends them away. Then Charlie is murdered by Indians. At the funeral his mother screams that Rachel is a 'dirty Indian'. Kelsey is captured and, tied on a horse with a rope round his neck, he is forced to tell his story, that Rachel was taken as a baby from the Kiowa camp after a massacre and raised by the Zacharys as their own. Charlie's father demands to know if this is the truth, but Mrs Zachary whips Kelsey's horse forward, hanging him before he can say more. Eventually Ben forces the truth from his mother, that Kelsey's story is true and that she took the Kiowa baby when her own had died. Cash, unable to bear the knowledge that his sister is an Indian, wants to send her away, but Ben refuses. The Kiowa return. Rachel wants to go with them to spare her white family, but Ben refuses to give her up. The Kiowa attack. Ben declares his love for Rachel and they embrace. Mrs Zachary is killed and Ben, Rachel and Andy are almost overcome when Cash returns to help save them. At the end Rachel comes face to face with her Indian brother and shoots him dead.

Ostensibly a pro-Indian Western, the film sets out to deny that blood is thicker than water. When Rachel refers to the Indians as 'my own kind', Ben replies: 'By blood, yes, but not by anything else.' Culture not birth is what matters to Ben, even if there are racists in the community. The Indians aren't treated as a viable alternative society, but merely as a threatening, and at times murderous presence. There's never any doubt that Rachel will stay a Zachary, despite her gesture of marking her forehead, Indian-style. If the racial politics are ultimately conventional, the film has great strengths, not least Lancaster's assured performance; when he cradles Rachel and tenderly whispers 'Little Injun', it's as good as John Wayne's 'Let's go home, Debbie' in *The Searchers*. Gish too is excellent, sitting outside on the prairie at night playing the 'Moonlight Sonata' on her piano to counter the weirdly disturbing flute music of the Indians.

Dir: John Huston; **Prod**: James Hill; **Scr**: Ben Maddow; **DOP**: Franz Planer; **Score**: Dimitri Tiomkin.

Viva Maria!
France/Italy, 1965 – 119 mins
Louis Malle

This doesn't seem much like a Western for the first hour. As a little girl, Maria (Brigitte Bardot) is trained by her Irish father to wage guerrilla warfare against the British. Now grown up, skilled with both guns and bombs, she battles against British imperialism in South America. On the run, she finds refuge in the caravan of a touring vaudeville entertainer, also called Maria (Jeanne Moreau). Under her tutelage, she learns about men and clothes and how to sing. One night on stage her clothes start falling off by accident. Turning adversity to advantage, the two women perform an impromptu striptease. Overnight they are a sensation, at each performance revealing a little more flesh. But their lives are changed when they witness poor peasants being oppressed by a wealthy landowner (Carlos López Moctezuma). When Maria II (BB) takes a shot at the landowner they are imprisoned, along with Flores (George Hamilton), a handsome revolutionary. Maria I (JM) falls for him and when he dies from his wounds, she promises to continue the struggle. Though at first reluctant to become involved, Maria II comes to the rescue of the guerrillas when they are pinned down by machine-gun and artillery fire, swinging through the trees like Tarzan and lobbing bombs at the opposing soldiers. Still clad in fashionable skirts, the two women lead a campaign of resistance which includes the capture of the army's special armoured train. But they are betrayed by the Church, which is in league with the forces of reaction. A Father Superior (Francisco Reiguera) tricks his way onto the train, produces a pair of six-guns and takes them prisoner. They are told they may leave the country if they sign a recantation, but they refuse. The two Marias are taken to the dungeons to be tortured, but the rack and other equipment prove decrepit with age. Instead they are taken out to be shot but saved at the last minute when the guerrillas overrun the presidential palace.

Louis Malle's film has much in common with the Italian Westerns being made at the same time, with its Mexican setting, rebellious peons led by foreign mercenaries, its frequently tongue-in-cheek presentation of violence and, not least, its anticlericalism. To this Malle adds his own Gallic wit and style, greatly assisted by the charm and allure of his two principals. The jokes, most of them visual, come thick and fast, most delivered in a throwaway manner as if to say, if you don't like this one there's another one coming. The grasping landlord proclaims himself a modern man, with electric light in his hacienda; he pulls back the curtains to reveal it is powered by toiling peasants cranking a huge dynamo by hand. The talents of the women's fellow vaudevillians are put to good use, the strong man pulling apart the iron bars of a prison, the conjuror's trained doves dropping hand-grenades, the acrobats vaulting barricades. Georges Delerue's songs are delightful, fitting accompaniments to a concoction as light and airy as a soufflé.

Dir: Louis Malle; **Prod**: Oscar Dancigers; **Scr**: Louis Malle, Jean-Claude Carrière; **DOP**: Henri Decaë; **Score**: Georges Delerue.

Wagon Master
US, 1950 – 86 mins
John Ford

A personal favourite among his films ('I think *Wagon Master* came closest to being what I wanted to achieve'), *Wagon Master* may seem at first sight a minor work in the John Ford canon. The film is very short, in black and white and has no major stars. But it distils much of the essence of Ford's view of the west. It begins, surprisingly for Ford, with a pre-credit sequence, in which the Clegg gang cold-bloodedly murder a bank teller in a hold-up. We then discover Travis (Ben Johnson) and Sandy (Harry Carey Jr), two amiable cowboys with a herd of horses to sell. They encounter a group of Mormons, led by the irascible Elder Wiggs (Ward Bond), whose tendency to fly off the handle needs to be constantly kept in check by the stern admonitions of Brother Perkins (Russell Simpson). The Mormons are being forced out of town by the marshal, and need someone to lead them to the San Juan Valley, where they will form an advance guard for later settlers. Having ascertained that Travis and Sandy neither drink, chew tobacco nor swear, Elder engages them to lead his wagon train.

On the trail they encounter a wagonload of show-people, marooned after their mule has run off. All of them are drunk, including the pretty Denver (Joanne Dru), the ham actor and quack doctor Locksley Hall (Alan Mowbray), the ageing Fleuretty Phyffe (Ruth Clifford) and drummer Mr Peachtree (the director's brother, Francis Ford). Despite this lapse, Elder agrees the show-people may travel with them as far as the California cut-off. Travis soon forms an attachment to Denver, though initially she dismisses him as a 'rube'. When after many miles across the desert they finally reach water, all plunge in. A celebratory dance is interrupted by the arrival of the Cleggs, on the run from the law. Uncle Shiloh Clegg (Charles Kemper) has been wounded in the hold-up and, seeing the legend 'Tickaboo snake oil and Lightning elixir. Teeth pulled and hair restored' on the side of his wagon, demands the quack doctor fix him up. The Cleggs take away Sandy and Travis's guns and hide out in the wagon train when a posse arrives in search of them. In the final sequence, the Mormons have to dig out by hand a track up the side of the mountains for their wagons and the vindictive Uncle Shiloh is about to drive their stock of seed corn over a cliff when Sandy produces another gun and the long-delayed shootout with the outlaws produces a just outcome.

This slight narrative is held together by lyrical shots of horses and pioneers in the desert, by some gentle comedy and most of all by music. At times the film is almost a tone poem, as the Sons of the Pioneers sing Stan Jones's music while the wagons roll slowly west, with Richard Hageman's musical arrangement of such Fordian anthems as 'Shall We Gather at the River?' providing back-up.

Dir: John Ford; **Prod**: John Ford, Merian C. Cooper; **Scr**: Frank S. Nugent, Patrick Ford; **DOP**: Bert Glennon; **Score**: Richard Hageman.

Warlock
US, 1959 – 122 mins
Edward Dmytryk

Based on Oakley Hall's intelligently written novel, *Warlock* is a classic
'town-tamer' Western, with a difference. The town is plagued by a gang
of local roughnecks, the San Pablo cowboys, who have frightened off a
series of sheriffs. When one of the gang shoots the local barber, the
townsfolk decide they have had enough and send for the legendary Clay
Blaisedell (Henry Fonda), despite the objections of the local judge, who
says that, as marshal, Blaisedell would have no legal status. Arriving in
Warlock with his friend, Tom Morgan (Anthony Quinn), Blaisedell makes
it clear that he will perform the task on his own terms, and forecasts that
the citizens will soon come to resent him for his methods. Soon Blaisedell
is in action, facing down some of the gang and imposing his authority.
Morgan's former lover Lily Dollar (Dorothy Malone) arrives in town, and
starts a romance with Johnny Gannon (Richard Widmark), a reformed
member of the gang who is now deputy sheriff, hoping this will help her
get revenge against Morgan for his former cruelty towards her. Gannon
is beaten up by the gang, one of whom pins his hand to the table with a
knife. But though wounded he overcomes two of them in a fight in the
street. Blaisedell suggests to Morgan that they can let Gannon take over
now. He has fallen in love with Jessie (Dolores Michaels) and wants to
settle down. Morgan cannot accept this and the two friends fall out.
Morgan gets drunk and Blaisedell is forced to shoot him. In his grief he
burns down the saloon and then goes into the street to face Gannon.
But though he draws he is unable to shoot. Throwing his guns aside, he
leaves town.

   At the heart of the film is the intensely emotional relationship
between Blaisedell and Morgan, unusual in a Western of this period. The
former, though courteous and soft-spoken, is reserved in his feelings and
remorseless in his handling of the town. 'All he knows is killing,' says Lily.
Morgan by contrast is a man who lives only for his friend, but his

pronounced limp seems indicative of a flawed personality. With his dyed blonde hair and dandyish clothes, Quinn communicates more than a hint of a gay sensibility, perhaps reinforced in his early brushing aside of the attentions of a saloon girl and his sneering remarks about marriage. When forced to explain his love for Blaisedell, Morgan says that 'He's the only person, man or woman, who looked at me and didn't see a cripple.' But his jealousy of Blaisedell's fiancée make it clear that something more

Clay Blaisedell (Henry Fonda) is watched by the friend who idolises him, Tom Morgan (Anthony Quinn), in *Warlock*

is at stake than his self-respect. Blaisedell's desire to withdraw from his occupation threatens Morgan's whole existence. His response virtually amounts to suicide as he gets drunk and descends for the fatal confrontation with his former friend, muttering Macbeth's words of nihilistic despair: 'Tomorrow and tomorrow and tomorrow. . .'. Blaisedell's tribute, creating a funeral pyre from the saloon, is a fittingly melodramatic finale.

Dir: Edward Dmytryk; **Prod**: Edward Dmytryk; **Scr**: Robert Alan Aurthur; **DOP**. Joseph MacDonald; **Score**: Leigh Harline.

Way Out West
US, 1936 – 65 mins
James Horne

All of Hollywood's great comedians seem to have had a Western in them, and Laurel and Hardy are no exception. The plot, such as it is, concerns the deeds to a goldmine, which the duo have to deliver to a pretty girl, Mary Roberts (Rosina Lawrence), living in Brushwood Gulch. But the rascally hotel-owner Mickey Finn (James Finlayson, mugging furiously), married to the ageing entertainer Lola (Sharon Lynne), plots to have Lola impersonate Mary and steal the deeds. When they realise they have been deceived, Stan and Olly burgle Finn's house in the middle of the night and after various disasters they retrieve the deeds and escape with Mary.

Stan Laurel has an unequal struggle to get Oliver Hardy aboard the stage in *Way Out West*

The story is, of course, a mere peg on which to hang a succession of Laurel and Hardy's best routines. Stan has some inspired business with a hole in his shoe, which he patches with a piece of meat that someone has pronounced as tough as shoe leather, only to be set on by a bunch of hungry dogs. Stan also discovers a miraculous ability to strike a light from his thumb, a gift which Olly spends the rest of the film trying to emulate, only to take fright when he succeeds. There are a few corny verbal gags ('What did he die of?' 'He died of a Tuesday, I think.'), but mostly it is perfectly timed sight gags, such as the business at the end with a rope and a pulley which results in their mule being deposited on the balcony of the hotel. Stan has an hilarious moment when Lola insists on searching him for the deed and, ticklish, he giggles hysterically. One of the gags, in which Stan pulls up his trouser leg in order to stop a stagecoach, you won't get unless you have seen Claudette Colbert hitching a lift in *It Happened One Night* (1934).

Best of all are the musical numbers. As the pair enter Brushwood Gulch they come across a group of singing cowboys (the Avalon Boys), with yodelling by Chill Wills (later to have a substantial part in *The Deadly Companions* [1961], Sam Peckinpah's first Western). Stan and Olly launch into a spontaneous dance, their dainty little steps a complete contrast to the rough-and-ready Western ambience. And then there is the moment everyone remembers, their rendering of 'The Trail of the Lonesome Pine', with Olly in a light baritone and Stan weighing in with a heavy bass (dubbed by Chill Wills) before Olly hits him on the head to send him into falsetto (dubbed by Rosina Lawrence). A moment of pure genius.

Dir: James Horne; **Prod**: Hal Roach; **Scr**: Jack Jevne, Felix Adler, Charles Rogers, James Parrott; **DOP**: Art Lloyd, Walter Lundin; **Score**: Marvin Hatley.

The Wild Bunch
US, 1969 – 138 mins
Sam Peckinpah

One of a number of films from the late 1960s which deal with the end of the west, *The Wild Bunch* is set in the early twentieth century during the Mexican revolution. An outlaw gang attempts one final hold-up before dispersing. But their attempted robbery of a bank in a small Texas town turns into a bloody fiasco as they walk into an ambush set by Deke Thornton (Robert Ryan), a former associate released from prison on condition he brings the gang to justice. Though the outlaws escape capture, they have failed to steal any money. Their leader, Pike Bishop (William Holden), organises a more successful raid, this time stealing rifles from the army, which they take into Mexico and sell to the brutal General Mapache (Emilio Fernandez). Things look to be going well until one of the gang, Angel, a young Mexican (Jaime Sanchez), is provoked into killing his former girlfriend, who is flaunting her affair with Mapache. The General's vengeance on Angel is savage. Attempting to rescue Angel in an act of perverse and suicidal heroism, Bishop leads the gang against Mapache's entire force. Many Mexicans are slaughtered before at last the gang are cut down in a hail of gunfire. Later Thornton arrives to survey the melancholy scene.

Though, as so often with Peckinpah's work, there were disputes with the producers about editing, this is an undisputed masterpiece, one of the towering achievements of the genre. It's a film of immense power, with several spectacular set-pieces, but also one of considerable psychological complexity. The opening massacre of the innocents, in which the townspeople are mown down in the murderous crossfire between the gang and their pursuers, brought a new level of visceral impact to the depiction of violence on the screen, but it is outdone by the final scenes of tragic sacrifice. Between these two events, the dynamics of the gang are explored in detail, Bishop attempting to instil some sort of honour among thieves while at the same time Thornton increasingly despairs of the stupidity and brutishness of the dregs he is obliged to work with.

But notions of honour seem outdated in a world where technology (motor cars, machine-guns) increasingly dominates and realpolitik and business (represented by the rapacious railroad) are more powerful than love and honour. If ultimately the wild bunch reveal the nihilism that lies

Walking towards the final confrontation in *The Wild Bunch*: Tector Gorch (Ben Johnson), Lyle Gorch (Warren Oates), Pike Bishop (William Holden) and Dutch Engstrom (Ernest Borgnine)

beneath their heroics, in comparison to Mapache and Harrigan (Albert Dekker), the railroad magnate, they are giants in a world of pygmies.

Though aesthetically the film is wholly Peckinpah's, it shows how influential the Italian Western had become. The Mexican setting, the amorality of the heroes (prepared to sell guns to the evil Mapache), the stylisation of gunplay all owe much to Sergio Leone's films of a few years earlier. But the end of the west, in which his heroes ascend to Valhalla, is a theme which by this time Peckinpah had made his own.

Dir: Sam Peckinpah; **Prod**: Phil Feldman; **Scr**: Walon Green, Sam Peckinpah; **DOP**: Lucien Ballard; **Score**: Jerry Fielding.

Winchester '73
US, 1950 – 92 mins
Anthony Mann

The first of the five Westerns that director Anthony Mann was to make
with James Stewart in as many years, and the only one in black and
white, *Winchester '73* is typical of the series in the extremes of emotion
displayed by the central character, who carries on his back the burden of
past trauma. It is the Fourth of July, 1876 and a genial Wyatt Earp (Will
Geer) presides over a shooting competition in Dodge City, the prize
being an especially fine example of 'the gun that won the west', a
Winchester repeating rifle. Taking part are Lin McAdam (James Stewart)
and Dutch Henry Brown (Stephen McNally). The enmity between them is
plain to see. After Lin wins the coveted rifle with a spectacular display of
marksmanship, it is stolen from him by Dutch. Lin and his friend High-
spade ('with a hyphen') Frankie Wilson (Millard Mitchell) take off after
Dutch and his companions, but before they can catch up with them,
Dutch has sold the gun to a disreputable Indian trader (John McIntire). In
the wake of Custer's recent defeat, the Indians are on the warpath; the
trader is murdered when he tries to sell them weapons and the chief
takes possession of the Winchester. Lin and High-spade are themselves
pursued and take refuge with a group of soldiers. Also in the camp are
Lola (Shelley Winters), a good-hearted saloon girl they have already met
in Dodge City, and her boyfriend Steve (Charles Drake). Lin offers his
experience of Indian fighting to the army sergeant (Jay C. Flippen),
informing him that Indians hardly ever attack at night: 'if they are killed
in the dark the Great Spirit can't find their souls'.

In the morning the company beat off the Indian attack. After Lin and
High-spade ride off, a soldier finds the treasured Winchester and the
sergeant gives it to Steve. Later, in town, Steve meets up with Waco
Johnny Dean (Dan Duryea), who taunts the cowardly Steve and kills him
in order to get the Winchester. Waco, with Lola in tow, meets up with
Dutch, who takes the gun off him. The two plan a bank robbery in

Lin McAdam (James Stewart) makes a forceful point to Waco Johnny Dean (Dan Duryea) in *Winchester '73*

Tascosa; Lin and High-spade arrive, and in the ensuing mêlée Waco is shot. As Dutch rides off into the mountains with Lin in pursuit, High-spade explains to Lola that the two are brothers, but that Dutch went bad and shot their father in the back. In a shootout among the rocks Dutch is killed and Lin finally takes back possession of the Winchester.

Early in the film James Stewart endures a beating, the first of many that he will suffer for Anthony Mann. It serves only to increase the fury

Lin feels towards Dutch, whom he pursues with a relentlessness that mystifies his easy-going partner. In a later scene he twists Waco's arm behind his back to force him to reveal Dutch's whereabouts, and the close-up of Lin's face reveals a man driven to the verge of hysteria. Stewart's performance gives the film a rare intensity.

Dir: Anthony Mann; Prod: Aaron Rosenberg; Scr: Robert L. Richards, Borden Chase; DOP: William Daniels; Score: Joseph Gershenson.

The Wonderful Country
US, 1959 – 96 mins
Robert Parrish

A minor miracle of a film, which fits Robert Mitchum's persona perfectly. Mitchum plays Martin Brady, who was born in the USA but has spent his life as a *pistolero* south of the border after killing his father's murderer. Entrusted by his Mexican patrons, the Castros, to bring a wagonload of guns down across the border, Brady breaks a leg when his horse shies and gets stuck in a small Texas town. The local army commander wants him to spy on the Mexicans, the captain of the Texas Rangers offers him a job and the army commander's wife Helen (Julie London), bored with army life, wants an affair. Brady tries to remain distanced from all who have demands on him, but when he is forced to shoot a man in a fight he is obliged to go back across the river to Mexico. When he goes to see Mexican general Marcos Castro (Victor Manuel Mendoza) he is humiliated and sent off to see the general's brother Cipriano (Pedro Armendaríz), who holds him responsible for the fact that the shipment of guns has not arrived. Protesting that he was laid up with a broken leg, Brady is then told that he must kill the General, who wants his brother's job of governor. Brady again encounters Helen, who is horrified that he has killed a man ('You're not complete without your machinery for killing,' she says witheringly). Influenced by her, Brady decides to refuse the task imposed on him by the governor and rides towards the north once more. He encounters Helen's husband, who has come south to join a joint attack against the Apaches, but who is mortally wounded. Helen tells Brady that, if he wants her, he must cross the river back north again. Escaping from the Mexicans, Brady's horse is killed. Leaving behind his gun and his sombrero, he once more journeys back into the USA.

'I haven't got a home,' Brady remarks at one point, but each side tries to claim him as their own. While he's recovering from his broken leg the doctor makes him take a bath (always a highly symbolic act in the Western, indicating a transition of some kind) and fits him out in

American clothes, but Brady obstinately hangs on to his sombrero. Back in Mexico, the governor orders him to dress more Mexican. The cross-border contrasts, and the sense that life down south is more real but more dangerous, anticipate Cormac McCarthy and are explored with even more subtlety in Tom Lea's original novel (Lea has a part in the film as a barber). Certainly Brady is more relaxed south of the border, which

South of the border, down Mexico way: Robert Mitchum (centre) in *The Wonderful Country*

is where his true friends are, but the film's presentation of Mexican life does not avoid all the usual clichés, with the authorities corrupt and their hangers-on swarthy and shifty. Mitchum brilliantly conveys a character who sees things for what they are and prefers to be his own man.

Dir: Robert Parrish; **Prod**: Chester Erskine; **Scr**: Robert Ardrey; **DOP**: Floyd Crosby, Alex Phillips; **Score**: Alex North.

Yellow Sky
US, 1948 – 98 mins
William Wellman

Based on a story by W. R. Burnett, whose novel *High Sierra* became a crime film with Humphrey Bogart and then *Colorado Territory*, a Western with Joel McCrea, *Yellow Sky* is a tightly plotted battle of wits. Gregory Peck is 'Stretch' Dawson, the leader of a gang of bank robbers who escape into a pitiless wasteland of salt flats. Almost dying of thirst, they miraculously stumble across a ghost town inhabited by a half-crazed old prospector (James Barton) and his granddaughter Mike (Anne Baxter). Among the gang is Dude (Richard Widmark), a gambler down on his luck who still carries a bullet in his chest from a man he cheated. Dude is obsessed with gold and persuades Stretch that the old man must have

Stretch Dawson (Gregory Peck) between his fellow bank robbers Walrus (Charles Kemper) and Bull Run (Robert Arthur) in *Yellow Sky*

some hidden away. But Dude and other members of the gang, especially Lengthy (John Russell), also lust after Mike. She is a tomboy who is adept with a rifle and when Stretch grabs it she punches him to the ground. Like the rest of his gang, Stretch is attracted to her; though he vows to protect her from the rest, he feels the need to show her who is strongest. 'Women got no business carrying guns, they're apt to shoot someone they don't mean to.' He wrestles with her and kisses her, but she responds by telling him he smells bad, and grazes his head with a well-directed shot. Eventually the old man confesses that he does have gold, but it is hidden in a mine. Stretch offers him a fifty-fifty deal, but once they have got the gold out of the mine Dude wants it all. Stretch sides with the prospector and Mike and in a final shootout in the ruined saloon Stretch comes out on top against Dude and Lengthy. At the conclusion Stretch rides into the town he robbed and hands the money back to the bank.

Marvellously shot by Joe MacDonald on location both in Death Valley and at Lone Pine in California (the site of many Westerns, including some of those which Budd Boetticher made with Randolph Scott), this is a highly skilled reworking of a familiar formula, of innocents pitted against a gang of hardened criminals. It is no great surprise when the Gregory Peck character proves that his heart is made of gold. Once cleaned up and shaved, he recounts to Mike and her grandfather his upbringing by sound farming stock and how he could read the Bible by the age of seven; only the Civil War has made him go bad. Nor do we doubt that Mike will eventually reveal her feminine side, confiding to Stretch that her real name is Constance May. On his return to town to restore the proceeds of the bank robbery, Stretch buys her a pretty little hat, symbol of her return to her natural state. But before this Baxter has given a spirited performance in a role which critics have compared to that of Miranda in Shakespeare's *The Tempest*, with the old prospector as Prospero.

Dir: William Wellman; **Prod**: Lamar Trotti; **Scr**: Lamar Trotti; **DOP**: Joseph MacDonald; **Score**: Alfred Newman.

Index

Page numbers in *italics* denote illustrations; those in **bold** inidcate detailed analysis

List of Illustrations

Whilst considerable effort has been made to correctly identify the copyright holders, this has not been possible in all cases. We apologise for any apparent negligence and any omissions or corrections brought to our attention will be remedied in any future editions.

The Big Trail, Fox Film Corporation; *Broken Arrow*, Twentieth Century-Fox Film Corporation; *Butch Cassidy and the Sundance Kid*, © Campanile Productions/© Twentieth Century-Fox Film Corporation; *Comanche Station*, © Ranown Pictures Corporation; *Cowboy*, © Phoenix Pictures; *Duel in the Sun*, © Vanguard Films; *El Dorado*, © Paramount Pictures Corporation/© Laurel Productions; *A Fistful of*

Dollars, Jolly Film/Constantin Film AG/Ocean Films; *The Good, the Bad and the Ugly*, P.E.A.; *The Great Train Robbery*, Edison; *Gunfight at the O.K. Corral*, Paramount Pictures/Hal B. Wallis; *The Iron Horse*, Fox Film Corporation; *Johnny Guitar*, © Republic Pictures Corporation; *The Law and Jake Wade*, Loew's Incorporated/Metro-Goldwyn-Mayer; *Little Big Man*, © Hiller Productions/© Stockbridge Productions; *The Magnificent Seven*, © Mirisch Company/© Alpha Company; *Major Dundee*, Jerry Bresler Productions/Columbia Pictures Corporation; *The Man from Laramie*, Columbia Pictures Corporation; *The Man Who Shot Liberty Valance*, Paramount Pictures Corporation/John Ford Productions; *The Missouri Breaks*, © United Artists Corporation; *Monte Walsh*, © Palladian Pictures/© Cinema Center Films; *My Darling Clementine*, © Twentieth Century-Fox Film Corporation; *Once Upon a Time in the West*, Rafran Cinematografica/San Marco Cinematografica/Euro International Films/Paramount Pictures Corporation; *One-Eyed Jacks*, Pennebaker Productions/Paramount Pictures Corporation; *Pat Garrett and Billy the Kid*, Metro-Goldwyn-Mayer; *Rancho Notorious*, © Fidelity Pictures; *Red River*, Monterey Productions/United Artists; *Ride Lonesome*, © Ranown Pictures Corporation; *Run of the Arrow*, © RKO Teleradio Pictures; *Shane*, Paramount Pictures Corporation; *The Shooting*, Santa Clara Productions/Proteus Films; *Stagecoach*, © Walter Wanger Productions; *The Tall T*, Producers-Actors Corporation; *Terror in a Texas Town*, Seltzer Films; *Warlock*, Twentieth Century-Fox Film Corporation; *Way Out West*, Metro-Goldwyn-Mayer; *The Wild Bunch*, © Warner Bros.; *Winchester '73*, © Universal Pictures Company; *The Wonderful Country*, © D.R.M. Productions; *Yellow Sky*, Twentieth Century-Fox Film Corporation.